Stillwater Trout Fishing

STILLWATER TROUT FISHING

John Bailey

The Crowood Press

First published in 1995 by
The Crowood Press Ltd
Ramsbury, Marlborough
Wiltshire SN8 2HR

British Library Cataloguing in Publication Data

A catalogue record for this book is available from the British Library.

ISBN 1 85223 860 7

All photographs by the author.
Line drawings by Paul Groombridge.

Typeset and designed by:
D & N Publishing
DTP & Editorial Services
Crowood Lane, Ramsbury
Marlborough, Wiltshire SN8 2HR

Phototypeset by FIDO Imagesetting, Witney, Oxon.
Printed and bound at The Bath Press.

CONTENTS

ACKNOWLEDGEMENTS 6

INTRODUCTION 7

1 A HISTORY OF STILLWATER TROUT FISHING.................10

2 THE QUARRY 15

3 TACKLE 25

4 FLY FISHING TECHNIQUE 38

5 THE EDGEFIELD EXPERIENCE................................51

6 THE JUMBO TROUT OF JURASSIC LAKE............................67

7 MANAGEMENT OF A TROUT FISHERY 73

8 THE LAKE AT LYNG 83

9 RESERVOIR FISHING 94

10 THE CHALLENGE OF LOCH FISHING 104

11 FEROX TROUT..124

12 FISHING FOR CHAR..138

13 A VIEW OF IRELAND 145

INDEX 157

ACKNOWLEDGEMENTS

There are a great many people who have helped me through my trout fishing career and to whom I shall always be grateful. More specifically here I would like to thank those people who have helped so unstintingly with this particular book: Alwynne Wheeler, who made the topic of trout food so simple and direct; Phillip Parkinson and Geoff Franks at Sportfish on the Welsh borders for all their strenuous efforts on my behalf; Michael Robbins, who is something of a legend on the trout waters of eastern England and Scotland; and Christopher Rowe, whose passion for fishing, power of imagination and lively intellect must be way beyond the norm.

Thanks also to Peter Stone, another legend – a man who has fished since childhood, rubbed shoulders with all the greats and made them all better anglers as a result; to Tom Boulton whose roots are in match fishing where he has excelled, an accomplished catcher of reservoir trout and an excellent teacher; to David Green, one of Great Britain's most practised stillwater fishery owners; to Terry Beale, fly tier and fly fisher who takes reservoir fishing and turns it into an art form; and to Malcolm Goddard who provides an excellent introduction to fly fishing on the lochs of Scotland. I must also thank Simon Gawesworth down in the west country for all his advice, and how I envy those who have been able to learn from his courses and guidance.

I would also like to thank two great friends who have helped in every way: Gordon Heath, owner of the Tomdoun Hotel, that haven for fly fishermen; and Richie Johnston, one of the most dedicated and skilled of the young Irish anglers now coming to the fore. Also Frederic Buller, not just for writing for us here, but for everything he has done to help me and my fishing over the last ten years or so; and his great fishing partner over on the Western Lakes, Des Elliot, who taught me how to dab, and who saved my life in a force 10 gale, too!

Finally I must thank Joy in particular because she suffered every type of abuse the weather could throw at her – and that can often be serious north of the Great Glen.

INTRODUCTION

Tintwhistle Reservoir had become settled in my memory as being grey, even slate-coloured, and immensely forbidding; so I was rather surprised when two or three years back I decided to visit the place and, virtually thirty years on, found the water much smaller and less formidable, and much more attractive than in my childhood memories. Perhaps these recollections result from the crippling disappointment I suffered there. . .

My success at Tintwhistle was almost unbelievable considering my complete lack of both knowledge and suitable tackle (more of which will emerge later in the book). Suffice it to say that according to the textbooks almost everything I did was wrong – and yet I caught fish. I was desperate to catch fish, and I worked like a dervish when I was on the reservoir. I began there when I was ten years old, and would often circumnavigate the whole place once or even twice during a day's fishing; I walked and I fished until I nearly wore myself into the ground. But fish did come, and so my mother would be persuaded to part reluctantly with the money for another ticket the following day: success achieved and rewarded.

So when was this huge disappointment? It was probably early May, and I remember that it was early evening, and that it was cold, wet and windy. None of these facts persuaded me to deviate from my normal method of using the dry fly; although there was nothing remarkable in this, as I simply didn't possess any wet ones. I remember exactly where I was standing: along on the left-hand bank, a quarter of a mile up from the dam wall just on the point where the stones give way to an outcrop of rocks. I had moved back almost to the car park in readiness for my parents' arrival, and was making a few last token casts just to see if I could boost the bag a little.

I always liked that area; there was usually a chance of a fish or two, and even the perch would come up and sup in something large, pulled across the surface. This I used to find very exciting, and is fish behaviour I don't think I have seen since. On this particular day, however, what happened was quite extraordinary; I can see it clearly even now, as though it were yesterday.

I had cast out almost as far as I could, the cast as I remember being somewhat wind-assisted by a breeze coming from right to left and a little from over my shoulder. I was using a small blue dry fly, about size 14 or 16, although I can't recall which pattern it was; I doubt I would have known its name then anyway. The amazing thing was that the fly had not even alighted on the water when a great black neb rose up to take it – battle was on. The fish took line off, right to the backing, but I never lost control and I never panicked. I just knew this fish was meant to be mine, and after fifteen minutes or so I had worked it very close indeed to the bank and could see it clearly – and it really was a true leviathan – cruising up and down, my tiny fly in its jaw. I edged backwards up the rain-sodden rocks, clawing to get at my landing net. I suppose that as I pushed back, the fish lunged down and the strain was just too much: the cast parted, and with a flick of the great tail the fish was gone. With it went my emotional stability: I sobbed out loud, and that was how my parents found me, howling at the rising moon.

I never forgot that fish, and my sense of betrayal was increased when the bailiff told me that a large brown trout had been washed up, dead, at the bottom of the reservoir close to his cottage. The weight was apparently 6lb 5oz, and it had in its jaws a small, unrecognizable fly. This just had to be my fish, a clear 5lb larger than anything I had ever caught before.

The stillwater trout fisherman is often in a world of his own.

In spite of the agony of losing that fish – and perhaps because of it – I carried on with my stillwater trout fishing in various pools and reservoirs here and there in the north-west region. I never did catch a trout anywhere near as big as that one from childhood, but a steady stream of fish around a pound came my way and I remained totally absorbed in the sport for several more years. Then Richard Walker and his book *Stillwater Angling* came into my life and exploded it, just as he did the lives of so many. For me, the most fascinating part of this classic work was the section devoted to carp fishing. I had been brought up, along with everybody else, to believe that carp were impossible to catch and so had always discounted them; yet here we were told otherwise. As a result, from about the age of fourteen my trout tackle was put aside as I became a carp angler.

Here is not the place to delve into controversy as to the various methods of carp, trout or sea fishing: each one has its own delights and certainly I have never regretted the years of carp fishing – indeed, I often go out with a carp rod to this day. In fact I believe that my angling life is far richer for this, as compared to those who only know one water or one species or one method.

My obsession with species other than trout continued through much of the 1970s; by this time I had moved to Norfolk and had become inspired by the huge river roach there. Sadly, by 1976–7 they were beginning to die out in numbers, and so once again I began to think about trout fishing. By then I was in my mid-twenties, and ten very happy trout-filled years were to follow. I resumed my apprenticeship at a small, relatively new lake in North Norfolk called Edgefield Hall, of which a great deal more later; suffice it to say for the time being that Edgefield, for me, still represents some of the most glorious evenings of my life, times that will never be forgotten.

So it was when I moved on to Lyng and the Norfolk Fly Fishers' Club. Their lake made just as favourable an impression on me, and the memories from those years as a club member come flooding in from all angles of my mind as I write now. But all things must pass, and in the late 1980s I decided that East Anglia had probably offered me about as much in trout fishing as it could; this in spite of my now frequent trips to Ardleigh Reservoir, and numerous one-off visits to Chew, Grafham and Rutland. Again it was a book that precipitated my change of heart: *The Fisherman's Bedside Book* by BB. This extraordinary work was published just post-war, and my own copy had been given to me in 1959. In the same way that a particular part of Richard Walker's book had motivated me, it was just one section of BB's that seized my attention: that on the ferox trout of Scotland.

By my mid-thirties I had realized that trout were in my blood for ever; but the time had come for me to pit my wits and the skills that I had learnt against a foe even more considerable: the mighty ferox. For that reason, I all but left Norfolk, giving up my membership of several clubs so that I could rent a bothy in the far north-west of Scotland and devote all my fishing time to the pursuit of this extraordinary sub-species of trout. I suppose in some way I knew that if ever I were to experience again that pulsating excitement I had felt all those years before on that Pennine reservoir when the six-pounder had broken my line and got away, then I was going to have to do something more dramatic than even Chew or Grafham would offer. The wild, rugged Highland lochs were now for me.

In this brief autobiography I have tried to show how intermittent my own angling career has been, in its learning curve of hiccups and starts, with sudden periods of acceleration. Nevertheless I hope it will serve as an adequate introduction to the glorious world of stillwater trouting, and inspire others to taste the sort of thrills that I have known for so many years. A large part of the book will be my own words, but there are many contributions by friends who are far more expert in certain areas than I could ever be.

This is important in angling: never think that you know everything, and never be afraid to go to a fellow fisherman for help and advice. A true and good angler will give it unstintingly, as I hope this book will, too. I hope it will also pass on the love of the mystery of trout, especially on a fly rod where the bond between man and creature is almost umbilical in its sensitivity and passion – that it will convey the exhilaration every angler feels at the scream of the reel, the swathe of spotted flank as a big fish turns – and the excitement and satisfaction that many years of trout fishing have given me and my friends. And I hope it will persuade both the beginner and trout fishermen of all experiences that every last ounce of effort is well worthwhile.

Stillwater trout offer a multitude of different waters, conditions and challenges.

1 A HISTORY OF STILLWATER TROUT FISHING

Men fished for trout in stillwaters many years ago, notably in Scotland and in Ireland, on the great and beautiful lakes of these two countries where trout grew wild and large. In the book *Loch Fishing* by A.C. Bridgett, published as far back as 1924, you will find the author saying, even then, that loch fishing was becoming more and more popular annually, also that even before the First World War, the pilgrimage north and west was gathering momentum. Certainly, from around the 1850s, the English began to move in these directions, and to pioneer new methods and more suitable tackle.

Any real innovation taking place in England itself tended to be in the rivers where, as history tells us, men such as Halford and Skues held sway, debating the different merits of dry fly fishing and nymph fishing. Certainly the real buzz of fly fishing, from the 1880s to the 1930s at least, centred around this issue, and clubs were broken up and friendships destroyed because of it. Anglers have always been competitive, but this period saw them at their most ferocious. However, this particular debate was not without its merits, and in fact the pioneers of stillwater trout fishing later in the century were greatly influenced by what Skues in particular had discovered.

Richard Walker was simply a Colossus. Having made his name with carp and coarse fish, Walker went on to help in the stillwater trout revolution, mastering all methods and techniques, and pioneering many of his own.

RESERVOIR FISHING

Soon, things began to change. From the middle of the twentieth century, population increases and the demands of industry and government planning all created a new angling dimension. Huge reservoirs were constructed to supply this developing world with water, and very soon these became stocked with trout. However, the enormous size and fertility of these waters meant that the fish were as wary as any wild ones, and took a great deal of catching; it also became apparent that traditional fly fishing techniques were not well adapted to the task of catching reservoir fish on a constant basis. Things had already started to change on older reservoirs such as Blagdon, but the 1950s and 1960s were largely exploratory days, and many anglers felt intimidated and demoralized by the sight of these vast expanses of water that stretched before them. A great deal of help was needed in this new branch of fishing.

In 1952 T.C. Ivens published his classic work, *Stillwater Fly Fishing*. It was in exactly the same era as Richard Walker's *Stillwater Angling*, and both these giants of the fishing world saw the demise of the river systems in what is a small overcrowded island. Both Ivens and Walker realized the increasing importance of the expanding reservoir and gravel pit complexes: they believed these to be the one sensible by-product of industrialized Britain for the angler, and history has proved them correct; stillwater angling for trout and coarse fish has proved to be the fastest growing area in modern angling.

Neither Ivens nor Walker sprang to the limelight from complete darkness: Walker leaned heavily on men such as W. T. Sheringham from the past, and on comrades such as Ingham, Taylor and Thomas from the present; and Ivens, in his book, drew from the traditional work that had been done on fly fishing. Thus he wrote in the preface to his 1952 book, that 'Skues' writing on nymphing has contributed something to my technique'. However, Skues could only have a limited amount of influence on vast waters such as Grafham, and his perfect little split-cane Leonard rod could not really offer that much when transported from the gentle features of the Wessex rivers.

ROD AND REEL DESIGN FOR RESERVOIR FISHING

Ivens realized that new weapons were necessary, especially for bank fishing on these inland seas; even at Blagdon pre-war, most fishing was done from boats in the old loch style that Bridgett would have recognized. Ivens, therefore, had to design rods virtually from nothing: the Ivens Ferrulite, the Ivens Superflyte, the Ivens Original, the Lake and the Ravensthorpe were all pioneering rods in a field that was demanding ever faster growth. These new rods needed to be married to new lines, too, so Ivens developed shooting and floating heads and began to recommend reels

capable of holding a hundred yards (90m) of backing – and these proved vital during the heady opening days of Grafham fishing when the rainbows offered sport the like of which stillwater anglers had never seen before. Ivens also alerted anglers to the complexities of the leader, and borrowed a great deal from the work done in America. Largely thanks to Ivens, therefore, the stillwater angler now had the basic tackle – but the technique to use it had not yet been mastered. Ivens again went to America and borrowed the concept of 'left-hand line acceleration' and casting. Ivens' casts travelled far and fast, his technique demonstrated in his book in a trend-setting sequence of nineteen photographs.

FLY DESIGN

Ivens may have read Skues on the subject of flies as he said, but he drew even more heavily from Skues' own disciple, Sawyer. Ivens continued the trend that Sawyer had put into progress, of rationalizing fly patterns, looking all the time for simplification and streamlining. Skues had concentrated on nymphing in the surface film or fractionally beneath it, and there was still a great deal of exploring to be done in this field: in 1906 Frank Sawyer was born for this task. From boyhood, the river was his fascination, offering him pike to snare, trout to poach, and countless mysteries that he sought from early years to unravel.

Frank Sawyer was determined to be a water keeper, and as early as 1928 he took control of a stretch of the Avon, upstream of Bulford, where he improved the river's efficiency by breaking up the gravels and chalking the water; but it was as a fly designer and tier that he is important to us now. Sawyer was a man of independent thinking, and he often disagreed with Skues; for example, one issue was the movement of hatching nymphs. Sawyer saw them struggle to hatch and thrust their thorax through to the air. Nothing to Sawyer was inert as it was to Skues, least of all a hatching nymph. Skues was not usurped by Sawyer, rather Sawyer realized that progress had to continue.

Bob Church was typical of the most successful stillwater trout anglers of today: he learnt his trade with coarse fishing, and then in the 1960s began to appreciate the tremendous excitement that was being discovered on the trout-rich reservoirs of the Midlands.

Sawyer began to develop his ideas in the *Fishing Gazette* and wrote widely on nymphing through the 1950s, obviously influencing Ivens in a big way. Ivens actually wrote that the ideal stillwater fly 'shall sink readily, its hackle fibre shall be soft and sparse and its wings very narrow and tend to lie low over the body'. These could almost have been Sawyer's words. Ivens was responsible for flies we still use today, such as the deadly Black and Peacock Spider. He also tied the early lures such as the Jersey Herd and the Polar Bear.

Above all, Ivens expressed constant regret at the clumsy and thoughtless manner in which so many bank anglers fished their fly, and he pleaded throughout his career for casting that showed consideration and artistry – the type of fishing in fact

that would have appealed to Skues on the Wessex rivers! Ivens was, of course, helped by the revolution in tackle-making; new rod, line and leader materials gave him the tools for this new craft of his, and step by step he began to explore every technological advance. Of course, the great influences on stillwater trout fishing as we know it today do not emanate from one man alone, and Ivens had his followers, his school. And if there was a motto for the Ivens school it would be adaptability and awareness of opportunity.

BOAT DESIGN

The most notable of Ivens' disciples was Dick Shrive, a quiet, modest man; although extremely

One of the all-time heroes: the late Dick Shrive, prepared for the Siberian winds that blow across our reservoirs.

inventive, he was only persuaded to make his ideas public by the pressure that Ivens and the then young Bob Church put upon him. Along with Ivens, he developed the technique of fishing the shooting head; but his greatest advances were in boat technique. The portable rudder revolutionized sunk-line fishing, and is still the only efficient way to approach deep water fly fishing on the large reservoirs today. Having sown the seed, the Northampton style of drifting inevitably followed, and so Shrive next invented the leeboard: for this effective drifting technique, a thwart board is clamped to the gunwhale and extended below the water in front of the bow angler; as a result the boat will cut across the wind. When the far bank is reached, the leeboard is changed to the other side and this brings the boat back again. In the days of the oar, the drift could be so extended ten times as long.

This exacting control of the boat allowed Shrive to pioneer his deep water, sunk-line tactics. When everyone else was fishing on the surface, Shrive was able to get his fly down deep, thus avoiding the stock fish of the upper layers, and where he used lures to capture the specimen fish. He would tie a Missionary lure, a New Zealand pattern originally, but modified to resemble roach, rudd or bream fly. The tying in whole and flat of the Silver Mallard Wing Feather was Shrive's innovation and attracted fierce takes to his flies, on the drop especially. Shrive learned his trade at Ravensthorpe, Hollowell, Eyebrook and later at Pitsford and Chew, when Grafham, Draycote and Rutland opened he already had a vast fund of experience; as a result his catches were outstanding and made sensational news.

PROGRESS TO THE PRESENT DAY

Today, the very best reservoir fly fishermen are probably the most competent fly anglers this country has ever seen. The work that Ivens, Shrive and Church have done over thirty years has been picked up and developed to such an extent that outsiders are flabbergasted by it. I remember some years ago when my own local

Not all the heroes are famous: this is an old portrait of Hector A. MacDonald, one of the greatest Scottish gillies and a particular expert on stillwater trout fishing. Here he holds a ten-pounder, taken – as legend would have it – on a fly.

club entered the Benson and Hedges qualifying match on Grafham. I got nowhere near the team, for all the members were considered to be locally expert – and yet even the pride of East Anglia was beaten out of sight by the Midland circuit men. Those who fished the likes of Rutland Water had developed skills way beyond those of the casual visitor, and quite simply the new generation – spearheaded by men such as Chris Ogborne – could catch in a variety of ways once never dreamed possible.

So there you have it: sixty years or more of development and exciting progress, building on foundations laid down in the last century by the giants fishing and writing then. This, I suppose, is what fishing is about, and there are bound to be leaders, men who insist that the sport can go forwards. This is why the influx of skilled coarse fishermen such as Bob Church into the stillwater trout scene was so important: they brought new ideas, new skills, and minds which were uninhibited by traditional ways of thinking.

The creation of these huge trout-stocked reservoirs has been a tremendous boon for fly fishing in this country, primarily because it means that trout fishing is no longer restricted to the rivers or to Scotland and Ireland and to areas that only the rich can afford. Trout has become the fish for everybody, regardless of background or income, and it is no wonder that the number of people able to cast a fly has risen dramatically from the 1960s onwards. Obviously, not all of these men could be fitted onto a handful of reservoirs, however large, and so gravel pits became stocked with trout, in fact they were often dug for that specific purpose. The situation today is such that every county has a plethora of stillwater trout fisheries, of every size and type, to suit every wish of every angler, no matter how deep his pocket.

Another unsung hero: John MacDonald (no relation to Hector), with an enormous brown trout.

2 THE QUARRY

Anglers and scientists have studied the trout for well over three hundred years, and records show that it is a fish which has always attracted attention and admiration. Professional biologists began detailed study as long ago as the eighteenth century, with the work of North and Albin; then men such as Yarrell, Day and notably Buckland followed in the nineteenth century, and Regan, Jones and Wheeler have continued this research in more recent years. At the height of its intensity, scientific study of the trout was probably best conveyed in the publication of *The Trout* by Frost and Brown, but a whole host of deeply informed, entertaining writing on the species has continued to appear, notably by Buller, Falkus, Downes, Giles and many others, all of whom have sought to understand this most enchanting species. Thus any reader who wishes to investigate the make-up of his quarry in the

greatest possible detail should have no worries as to where to look! Here, however, it is probably best to give a more practical, as opposed to scientific, introduction to the trout we are all likely to encounter in our adventures in this country.

IDENTIFYING TROUT SPECIES

The Brown Trout
The brown trout is the traditional trout of British waters, although there are many biological forms which have been traditionally declared as subspecies. The Reverend Houghton, writing in 1879, distinguished six different varieties, and writers after him 'found' a great many more. Colin McKelvie in his *A Game Fisher in Ireland* (1989) describes the excellent sonighan trout of Lough Melvin:

Portrait of a beautiful brown.

The sonighan is a bright, lively little trout barely running to more than 1–1¾lb, and a good average would be just under one pound. The basic coloration is olive shading to silver on the flanks, and the fishes [sic] body is deep in the flank and the head is small and neat. Sonighan are heavily marked with large, dark spots, their tails are especially broad and square and they have distinctive dark and rather elongated pectoral fins ... there is a good deal in the appearance and fighting abilities of these sonighan to suggest some affinity with sea trout, and at one time it was suggested that these were indeed land-locked sea trout stemming from some ancient race. But since Melvin has a direct and easy link with the sea, the term 'land-locked' simply will not do, and the most recent scientific studies have concluded that the sonighan are actually a distinct species of brown trout, of very ancient origins, which have descended from primaeval stock which colonized Lough Melvin in the immediate aftermath of the last Ice Age.

Whether this rather highbrow biologist's debate is likely to concern the man who just wants to catch anything with spots and an adipose fin I am not sure, but it is as well to know that the controversy exists.

For me, as indeed for many, brown trout have great sentimental appeal. There is a tremendous range of fish within the species, from the slim wild brownie in a lochan at two thousand feet, to the awesome ferox of a vast, deep Ice Age loch, with every variation in between. Even a recently stocked brown trout with a stumpy tail is still somehow appealing in some way; perhaps it is the buttery yellow stomach or the profusion of spots – or maybe it is simply British nostalgia.

The brown trout is a survivor, and it has a colossal range: I have fished for it in waters as far east as Kashmir, as far north as the tundra belt and as far south as Bosnia, and that doesn't even touch the outskirts . . . oh, for a chance to catch those browns of New Zealand or Montana or South Africa; and how about the brown of the Falklands, the one that decided to go to sea, with results that have astonished the angling world?

This picture shows just how different brown trout can be, even from the same water. Notice the difference in shape and spotting between these nine trout.

The head of a big brown trout. The number of scales on the gill-flap and the manner in which the mouth extends past the eye are both good ways of distinguishing big trout from small salmon.

In short, the wild brown trout is a magnificent fish and has become every connoisseur's favourite. It is still the most sought-after fish in the British Isles, just as it is the ultimate for many game anglers all around the world.

The Rainbow Trout

By contrast, rainbow trout are seen – probably unfairly – as rather brash fellows, with little of the subtlety and sophistication of browns. In part, I fear, this is because more of them originate from America than anywhere else, since it was the McCloud river in northern California from where they were taken to Britain, Europe, Australasia and even Japan over a century ago.

The rainbow rarely breeds successfully in Britain – although it probably manages to breed more successfully than we often tend to think.

Most rainbows, however, are stocked fish, and this is bound to have some effect on their appeal: the spirit of the wild is just not inherent in rainbow as it is in browns. To many people this is nonsense, and the rainbow has to be considered a far more swashbuckling character altogether, and a lot more pleased to give sport whenever he possibly can than the brown, who does tend to sulk when conditions are not to his liking.

Thus arguing in their favour, rainbows often shoal more readily than browns, a fact that gives bursts of sport which can liven up the dullest of days; furthermore they have a wider feeding range and are therefore caught through a greater part of the day than browns. They also tend to rise more freely to the surface or just beneath it, and are not nearly as wary as browns of sun or bright light. They roam further over much larger

The ultimate rainbow: the great steelhead of North America. This magnificent fish weighed in excess of 20lb and fought for over an hour.

territories so there is always a chance of making contact with a fast-moving fish. Finally, in my experience, rainbows will often make their minds up more quickly: a brown often needs to see a fly several times before it decides whether to take it or not, whereas a rainbow will give an immediate and often positive answer if it feels in the mood. Of course we are talking about fish here, and any discussion of 'character' is bound to run into problems: at the end of all this, we still need to fish carefully, thoughtfully and with optimism whichever the species we are pursuing.

The Brook Trout or Char

When the stillwater trout boom spilled over from the reservoirs into smaller waters in the seventies and eighties, a vogue for exotics appeared. Various hybrid trout made their appearance, accompanied by a great deal of hype and publicity, but the most interesting introductions were those of American brook trout. Now, the brook trout is actually a char, one of those Arctic salmonoids

found in high latitudes and generally restricted to cold waters. But the char is a troublesome fish to categorize, and there is little common agreement amongst biologists as to which char are actual species and which are sub-species. In fact some scientists claim that there are up to a dozen noticeably different chars, for example the lake trout and the Dolly Varden in America and, of course, the brook trout that made its appearance in this country.

The brook trout that I was lucky enough to catch in the early eighties were interesting fish, quite recognizable as char with their white-edged fins and unique spotting patterns – or to be more accurate, speckling – on the skin. Also, those that I encountered in half-a-dozen different waters tended to lie quite deep and maintain shoal formations, much as you might expect a native shoal of Arctic char to behave in Loch Ness.

At the time most of us enjoyed the challenge, or at least the difference that brook trout offered; but in such alien environments the fish did not feed very eagerly or fight very well, and once the novelty wore away, there was not a great deal of demand for subsequent re-stocking. In fact, in all the waters in which I found them originally, not a single fish now remains, the fishery managers having found them quite unprofitable.

The Stillwater Salmon

This was rather the case with the stillwater salmon, great jumbos of fish placed in small fisheries where conditions were as unlike the salmon's true environment as it is possible to imagine! In the waters in which I encountered them, they did cause a commotion when they first arrived, and seeing those great fins whale around and crash out like silver logs was impressive at first. However, once again it soon became obvious that many of these salmon were not going to thrive because they were not in their preferred environment: they

sulked, or lost condition, and some eventually died, causing embarrassment – financial and otherwise – to the fishery owners.

Even for the punter, the land-locked salmon was a very mixed blessing. In those waters where catches were paid for by the pound and release is not allowed, a salmon could prove a severe financial liability because a single fish could consume all the available money and more, in that it might outweigh by a considerable amount an average day's catch of four or more nice rainbow trout. On at least one of the fisheries where these salmon were stocked, it was possible to take out insurance *against* actually landing one! A ticket costing £2 ensured that any stray salmon could be taken home free of charge, so that at least the angler could work his lure without too much worry should it be seized by a leviathan!

Jumbo browns are now being produced, although they will never take the place of the wild fish.

Coping with Coarse Fish

So for all the above reasons and no doubt more, on most of the stillwaters of England at least, the game fish that will probably be encountered will be either browns or rainbows. Notice the description 'game': in many waters there also co-exist coarse fish, often regarded as undesirables. This attitude is understandable, especially if you have been flogging the water for several hours, register a take, and then land something quite obviously inedible! However, it is still a shame, especially when you consider the attractions of at least one of the more persistent 'sinners', the perch. Perch often proliferate in reservoirs especially, and Chew Valley is a prime example – Chew is also the water where I personally have seen very fine perch up to 3lb caught, landed and then kicked onto a heap where their shoal members are slowly suffocating. This disregard for fine fish is unwelcome in itself, but it is particularly damaging when you consider how much anglers are in the public eye when fishing at such places where the banks are continually walked and binoculars scan every last bay in search of rare birds: here every slight misdemeanour simply heralds its crime.

Like perch, bream, roach and even carp will all fall for a fly from time to time: unless the rules forbid it, let me suggest here that they are enjoyed for what they are, and that their own particular merits are appreciated. I remember well an angler playing a 14lb mirror carp that had sucked in a small white lure, and being given the thrill of his life. That fish took fifty minutes to land, and the angler was wise enough to appreciate the battle he had experienced down to every last pulsating second.

FOOD AND LIFESTYLE

Most of us accept that there is more to catching trout than pulling lures back through the water, lures that are probably attacked for a variety of reasons; we recognize that it is also necessary to start looking at what food the trout eats naturally in its environment. Then we can wonder about how to imitate this, and so catch trout in a way that will almost certainly bring ultimate satisfaction.

If you analyse the foodstocks of any stillwater you will find them enormously varied and abundant, especially in midsummer when life is at its most vibrant. Unless they are particularly preoccupied, it is likely that most trout feed on a great many things; therefore many artificial flies, as long as they are small, dark and move in a roughly convincing fashion, will be taken by a trout, thinking these to be a natural food item of some sort or another. This vagueness, however, does not mean that there are not several clearly recognizable forms of trout food, foodstuffs that probably make up the backbone of a normal trout's diet.

Alwynne Wheeler, formerly of the Natural History Museum and author of many books on fish and their biology, has this to say:

> As for trout food in a stillwater, one could say a lot. It all depends on the size of the trout – little ones may feed heavily on water fleas if there are any in the lake, whereas big fish will feed heavily on small fish. The answer also depends on the size of the lake and its fauna because trout, like most fish, will exploit whatever is abundant and easy to catch. But with all the *caveats* removed, I would go for a league table of *trichoptera* – especially caddis larvae, fishes, *chironomid* pupae, *ephemeroptera* larvae, insects and so on falling into the water or getting blown in by the wind, and snails. I think, however, that the first three will always head the table, and these should be looked at in great detail.

Trichoptera

The dominant physical characteristic of this family group of flies is that they have roof-back wings, that is, they are large and slant, and so in profile look like a roof. The life-cycle of these flies starts as an egg, then moves to lava, to pupa and so to the adult and the sedge or caddis stage; the latter are probably the most representative of the family. The sedges, or caddis, are very variable in size but tend to be large as compared with other English fly forms – which probably makes them particularly attractive. The adults have an erratic flight pattern, and trail very long antennae, so they are quite easy to recognize.

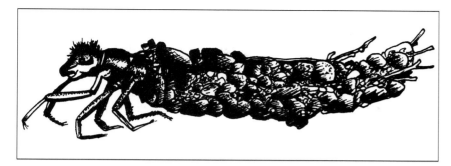

Fig. 1 *The caddis larva in its case built of shingle, sand grains, twigs and whatever else it can find on the bottom.*

The female will lay several hundred eggs which stick together to a piece of vegetation. These hatch out to become the common caddis larvae, which then proceed to build themselves protective homes from sand, twigs or leaves or any other bit of vegetation that they can find. These larvae spend their lives on weed or on the bottom of the lake until they break out of their case and either swim to the surface or make their way up any piece of weed-stem. When the surface is reached, the adult sedge will try to fly by flitting its way across the water until enough momentum is reached. The flies then mate on the land, and the female goes back to the water to lay her eggs and die.

There are many caddis imitations for fishing sub-surface, such as stick flies for example; these are all effective throughout the season, especially fished slowly and deep. Sedges are most likely to hatch during very settled weather conditions, and especially towards the evening. Probably the Invicta has long been one of the most reliable of imitations, although there are many patterns on the market.

Fish

The whole host of tiny fishes that swim in most of our stillwaters – roach and bream fly, small perch, sticklebacks and minnows – are all prime food fodder for the growing, inquisitive trout, and at times both rainbows and browns will slash into shoals of small fish as though their lives depended on it.

Richard Walker designed his Polystickle to imitate the stickleback, but many of the other white, green or silver lures on the market are probably just as effective. Certainly, it makes sense to try a fish imitation when the trout are quite obviously feeding off fry or herding up sticklebacks, and takes can be dramatic.

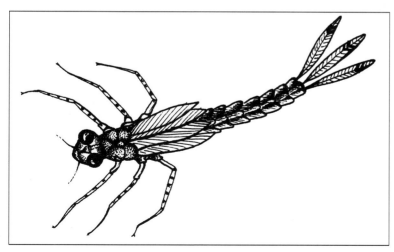

Fig. 2 *The damsel-fly nymph.*

Chironomid Pupae

These flies, belonging to the *Diptera* family, are very important flies to stillwater trout fishermen: they are the midges, the non-biting, mosquito-shaped insects that belong to a family with a vast variation of size and colour. These midges occur pretty well everywhere in the United Kingdom, even on slow-moving stretches of river. They probably hatch most days of each year, and because they are so common, you are almost certain to find some evidence of some form of midge life in every trout autopsy. The eggs are usually deposited on the surface of a lake and they drift around until they hatch or become attached to reed or other flotsam.

The eggs hatch into larvae which live in the mud at the bottom of the lake. They form great big colonies and inhabit both shallow and deep water. They vary in size, the normal length being ½in (12mm) although this can sometimes be double. In colour they can look almost transparent, or green or brown, or quite a vivid red; this red version is probably the most common, and is the reason for the larvae often being called 'bloodworm'.

The larvae develop quickly into the next stage, the pupae: shape and appearance change and they develop a hunchback and white fluffy gills at the head.

When conditions are right and the hatch is on, vast numbers of chironomids leave the mud together, and wriggle and sway their long and dangerous journey to the surface. This can take some time, and trout will often be feeding on rising midges and rising midge pupae before you see any evidence of the rise. Sometimes pupae get to the surface but are not ready to hatch, and these can drift long distances, constantly vulnerable. Once

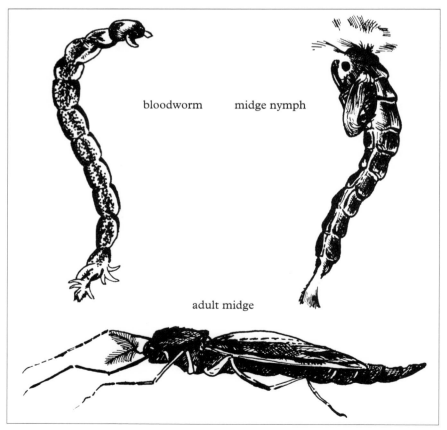

bloodworm   midge nymph

adult midge

Fig. 3 *The bloodworm, one of the most common organisms in any stillwater. These are frequently red, though not always, and are gorged by every fish species, not trout alone.*

Fig. 4 *The midge in its nymph stage, commonly called a 'buzzer' before it hatches, usually on warm, still summer evenings. However, there are buzzer hatches at most times of the year.*

Fig. 5 *The adult midge has emerged.*

hatched, the adult midge will often sit on the water and be taken as a dry fly by the trout; surviving midges gather over the land, and after mating, the female returns to the water to lay her eggs.

The sight of trout rising to hatching midges is most exciting and quite unmistakable, and the artificial fly most often used is one or other of the various different 'buzzers', sparsely dressed flies tied to imitate the hatching nymph as closely as possible.

Ephemeroptera Larvae

These flies have upright, V-shaped wings; the best examples are mayflies and olives. They are commonly considered a river fly, but healthy populations can be found on many lakes.

The eggs hatch into nymphs, which can live under the water for anything between six and eighteen months; some of them burrow into mud and silt, whilst others crawl around the bottom. Eventually the nymphs make their way to the surface where they hatch into flies, known as duns. These dry their wings until they are capable of flying away, when they will complete their brief life-cycle; they have no means of feeding, so they have to develop very quickly. The skin splits and the final, mature spinner emerges; these are delicate creatures that dance about in the air, then mate and finally lay their eggs, thus completing the cycle. All the spinners eventually die, falling with wings outspread on the water surface when the trout will frequently gorge themselves.

Other Foodstuffs

This is a very brief and simple analysis of trout foodstuffs. However, when selecting artificials, it is important in the early stages not to be too elaborate, nor to be too intimidated by the mass of food in the larder; keep things simple! Wheeler mentions wind-blown food, and one of the most prominent of these is the prosaic daddy-longlegs, especially in the later summer when trout rises to these can be dramatic.

Alwynne also mentions the snail, which in its many forms is very important in the diet of all stillwater trout throughout the country. There are all manner of forms of snail, but the most sig-

Fig. 6 The snail in one of its many differing forms, most of which are favourite trout food.

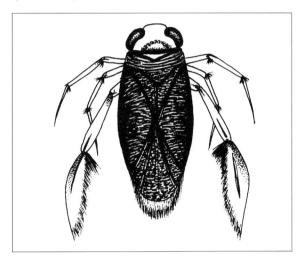

Fig. 7 The corixa or water boatman.

nificant is almost certainly the common wandering snail; this grows to about ¾in (19mm). As regards artificials, probably the black and peacock spider is as fair an imitation as possible, and no doubt when it is fished slow and deep, trout will take it as a general snail-type.

Another food source is the corixa, a small bug about ½in (12mm) long, with a dark shell and a whitish under-body. It will shoot to the surface to take in oxygen, and then make its slow and lumbering way back to the stillwater bed where it hides, inviting predation as it goes. There are several patterns of artificial corixa on the market, all most effective at certain times of the year – especially in August and September, in my experience

Fig. 8 *The shrimp, common in most stillwaters.*

– providing they are worked with a certain amount of thought and control.

Trout will also eat the freshwater shrimp, which can usually be found in any stillwater feeding area.

These small, golden-haired creatures are represented by many different artificials, and most work at some time or another, especially when worked well in, or as close to weed as possible.

Daphnia should also be mentioned, the water-fleas that rise to the surface in vast numbers, especially in cloudy weather. Trout, as all freshwater fish, tend to become heavily preoccupied with these daphnia conglomerations, which can look almost like the Milky Way in the water. However, trout can be tempted when daphnia feeding, unlike bream or tench, especially by orange or green-thoraxed pheasant tails or small orange nymphs. Daphnia will generally be driven before the wind, so look for bays where the waves are blowing in, or the corners of dams where wave action has been intense for a good few hours at least.

Irish dappers catch the mayfly.

3 TACKLE

I am indebted to Philip Parkinson and Geoff Franks of Sportfish for their help and advice in compiling this chapter. Sportfish is a game fishing mail-order company, so Philip and Geoff obviously have a wide overview of all the tackle available today for the trout fisherman.

RODS

The price range for rods is enormous, at the bottom end of the market the cheap, but reliable and serviceable piece of tackle that would serve a person very happily for years and never let them down, at the top end the luxury model with a very big price tag indeed.

My advisers were quite decided that any stillwater trout fisherman should have a standard 9ft 6in medium-actioned rod able to carry any line weight between 6 and 8, and considered that the Daiwa Whisper range offered the very best value in the economy rod class. They both testified to its strength, and to the fact that anybody buying the Daiwa would be very unlikely to tire of it; and

Most treasured possessions: a collection of old fishing tackle.

The range of fly fishing rods is endless.

certainly there is no point in buying a budget rod, using it for a year or two and then finding that it is sub-standard.

Otherwise, the Bob Church range is to be recommended, offering very sound value for money and proving particularly useful to anglers wanting to throw lures about larger waters. There is also the Shakespeare Oberon range, always very popular indeed, and the better Shimano rods, especially the new Stradic, which my advisers felt would prove extremely useful at the top end of the price-conscious market.

Amongst the higher priced rods, there is nothing currently on the market to beat the Sage models, especially for rods at around 9ft 6in for normal fishing or at 10ft for lure fishing. These rods are expensive, but are worth every penny. There seems to be a growing conviction that the brand to be aspired to is an American product when it comes to the very top range of fly fishing equipment. The Sage is a quality product, and its performance is just as stunning as its looks. To handle, the Sage rod is light, delicate and precise, but doesn't feel in any way stiff or unyielding; yet Philip assured me there was real solid casting power there. Of course, the feel of a rod and its beauty are both subjective impressions, and there are no true objective yardsticks; however, the Sage rod is undoubtedly made of the highest quality fibre, and simply oozes class.

I suppose a major question is whether a fishing rod can ever really be worth several hundred pounds; after all, we have already determined that the Daiwa more than does the job demanded of it – and as Geoff said, you can drive to London in an old Ford or a brand new Mercedes and both will get you there. But surely the point is that the actual *fishing* is only part of the sport's charm, and that there is also great pleasure to be had in using fine tackle that gives instant and eternal satisfaction.

There are also rods with specialized abilities because the range of stillwater trout fishing open these days is so vast that one rod will probably not be enough to cope with every situation that will be faced. Indeed, the fly rod manufacturers of today offer a vast range, setting out to cater for every single possibility. However, I was recommended the 10ft rod from the Sage range, designed to carry a weight 5 line; this is clearly a beautiful rod for fine tippets, when a dry fly or a nymph has to be placed with consummate delicacy at some distance.

Also, a longer rod of around 11ft 3in, probably carrying a no 8 or even no 9 line, might well be needed when boat fishing on big, rough water such as Lough Mask in Ireland. With a rod of this length the top fly can be run across the waves with great ease.

Then there are the travel rods, the multiple-piece affairs that the travelling businessman can simply slip inside his suitcase and forget about, but which are there if the opportunity to fish ever arises. Shakespeare make marvellous six-piece rods, up to 9ft 6in in length, at very reasonable prices.

I brought up the question of rods for jumbo trout on the smaller fishery that once at least was so popular. Philip thought it might be wise to look for a heavier rod capable of carrying heavier line to give a little bit more power; Geoff, however, disagreed with this and felt that the normal tackle would be more than sufficient – he considered that the onus was rather more with the angler, who would simply need to exercise more patience when playing a big fish and realize that time was essential to tire it out. In fact, he felt that a big rod with heavy line might simply pull the fly right out of a very big fish's mouth.

REELS

Many would say that the reel for the fly fisherman is only really a storage mechanism. However, I don't suppose this is quite true when very big fish in deep waters are being discussed, because then the reel must have the capacity to give line *and* offer some form of control to the angler. In fact it is this control that is one of the most important considerations, and one which has dominated the minds of marketing executives for some time. In essence, the choice is between disc-drags and click-drags. The disc is the 'new' thing, but in many circumstances it is often irrelevant, and the older, cheaper click will probably do just as well. However, we are once again looking at that intangible consideration, pride of ownership; and once again, there is little doubt that a beautifully crafted reel is infinitely more pleasurable to use than a cheap, tacky object.

At the bottom, standard end of the market is the ubiquitous Rimfly reel. This is metal, durable and simple, and it works: I personally have used Rimflies in virtually every part of the world, and have never had any problems with them. They are also inexpensive – which should excuse the fact that they are not really classic pieces of engineering.

Slightly up the scale is the Leeda LC system, reels with a graphite composite body and a plastic spool. These are light, efficient, and come offering a cassette system, very useful for the man who wants to take a number of lines with him.

At around the same level is the Dragonfly, also quite reasonably priced. This offers disc-brakes with a metal spool and a graphite back, and it looks good and behaves very well. The general

Rods, reels and line are the obvious; and remember the camera, and even the echo-sounder if you are being scientific.

trend is towards cassettes at the moment, so bear this in mind when choosing a reel. This brings us to the top end of the market, where the best reels are considered to be the System 2 reels made by British Fly Reels in Falmouth – robust, reliable and high quality. These offer a highly adjustable disc-brake for the control of running fish and for rim control; there is also the counter-weighted handle if you want it. All in all, the System 2 is a durable reel with an excellent check; it is well built and the sound simply purrs – the perfect reel to team up with the Sage rod.

Of course there are others: the Orvis Battenkill, and at the very top of the range, the Swedish Loop reel, often described as the ultimate fly reel in terms of function and design. You really need to see this reel to understand it – and once seen never forgotten! It is extraordinarily light and smooth, in part due to the fact that it runs on ball races; a remarkable design and a pleasure to use, with a drag system second to none. Put one of these on the Sage rod and you will have the ultimate team!

BACKING

As far as most stillwater trout anglers are concerned, the backing never really comes off the reel at all; it is simply there to bulk up the spool, and to provide a safety net if occasionally the fish of a lifetime comes along. The cheapest backing is simple and rot-proof and will probably do for years. Upgrade a little bit and there is dacron, a braided material of fine diameter. Dacron is smooth, strong and totally reliable, so if you are fairly confident that the backing is going to be in use at least some of the time, then it pays to step up a little.

Nowadays backing also comes in high visibility colours, which do prove useful if you are playing a big fish in a large and deep water: at least you can see in what direction, roughly, the fish is running.

FLY LINES

This must be one of the biggest choice areas, for there are many companies offering countless different designs. To start with, every stillwater trout angler undoubtedly buys a floating line and a medium sinking line. Then there are the more specialized lines, such as the intermediate; this is really useful in a flat calm, as it sinks just beneath the surface film and leaves no line-wake on the retrieve. And at the other end of the scale we have the super-fast sinking lines, so useful in the early season and during really hot weather spells when the fish are down deep.

Today 70 to 80 per cent of the lines that Sportfish sell are weight-forward design. The American market is even more biased towards these distance casting lines, to the extent that both here and across the Atlantic the old double-taper line is steadily disappearing.

When choosing lines, all sorts of considerations come into play, not least the length of the head of a shooting line. Simply put, the longer the head, the further you will cast, although a long head does cause casting problems; in fact you must be very competent indeed to aerialize a 20yd (18m) headed line. This is a problem that most beginners do not appreciate: that they have to choose the right line for their rod and for their casting abilities. If the line they choose is too heavy, then the rod feels soft; but if their line is too light, the rod will be stiff. Thus when choosing a fly line it really does pay to take experienced advice, and to go to great pains to make sure the right decision is made.

As usual, let us begin at the cheaper end of the market. Having said that, it does not pay to go too cheap when it comes to fly lines, because they are absolutely essential for efficient casting and good fly presentation. Another problem is that lines can go sticky in warm weather, and it is vital always to have a line that is supple as well as smooth. It was also Philip's opinion that you paid a lot extra for a small step up in performance, and that this was for design – for special tapers, say – rather than for line quality. Thus the customer who wants a specialized line is really paying for the research involved and is subsidizing a line that will not sell in great volumes.

There is constant research into fly lines: it is a world that never stands still – for example, scientific anglers are continually updating their lines, even looking for intermediates that will be totally invisible under water. For the less discriminating angler, however, better priced lines at the budget end of the market are those made by the Shakespeare company; and at the higher end are the lines produced by Scientific Anglers, or Cortland.

LEADERS

For many years now, The traditional leader material has been of nylon line. Again traditionally, most serious anglers make up their own tapered leaders rather than buying expensive manufactured ones. However for the single fly, or when presentation must be absolutely immaculate, the knotless tapered monofilament leader takes a lot of beating. But when a team of flies is going to be used, most anglers will tie a leader of different, tapering line strengths and leave tippets to take the drop flies. The only real option to this typical set-up is the appearance on the market of the leader link: these are minute silver rings, and using them avoids the necessity of bloodknots. Tie the tip of your leader on to one of those 2mm-diameter, very strong silver rings, and then tie your tippet length to the ring. Despite their apparent fragility, these are 100 per cent reliable, and weigh so little that they don't affect the turnover or the leader's floating or sinking properties. They are absolutely perfect when it comes to tying on a dropper, and offer a much quicker system so that you end up with more fishing time, clearly an advantage, especially when the rise is really on.

Another innovation that should be discussed is the pre-stretched, very fine nylon line, Drennan leading the way with Double Strength. Double Strength created a sensation in the coarse fishing market, especially when it first appeared, and most anglers flocked out to buy spools of the stuff. However, disillusionment followed rapidly when it was found that Double Strength had many irritating disadvantages. Nevertheless, our coarse fishing brothers have realized that there is a

There is a huge range of leaders and tippets.

compromise, and that Double Strength does have its place as long as it is used with thought and care in specific situations. Exactly the same can be said of Double Strength in the fly fishing world.

The main problems with Double Strength when it comes to fly fishing are that it does not sink particularly well, and that knot strength is frequently affected. Also – and this is my own major criticism of Double Strength – it offers no tolerance whatsoever, and the slightest bruise on it can easily result in a lost fish. Geoff recounted a recent trip with a friend at Chew: the friend used a leader of Double Strength and Geoff had a traditional monofilament. The friend had about double the takes, but lost at least half the fish; so although the action for Geoff was less frantic, at least every fish hooked was landed. And that should be the way for all fly fishermen, as there is nothing clever in hooking fish and then letting them go free with a hook and nylon dangling from their mouths.

However, when all this is said, there are situations when very fine Double Strength can offer advantages in presentation: perhaps when using really tiny flies, when the fish are at their most discriminating, a spool of Double Strength will more than pay for itself.

The major innovation in leader material is without doubt that of braided line, Airflo being the main brand, with Orvis not far behind. The reasons that braid has caught on are simple: first, nylon leaders tend to be stiff and unyielding, whereas braid is perfect in its suppleness. Thus a typical braided leader will start out with twenty-four strands in the butt, but these strands will be cut out as the leader progresses, and the rough ends will be melted back into the line. As a result, many anglers find it easier to get a perfect turnover with a braided line.

Second, braid allows far greater and more exact depth control. You can choose the density of braid that you want, and you will then know exactly how it will sink or float. Also, because the braid is slightly rough, you can rub it with tungsten powder; the more tungsten powder on the line, the quicker it will sink. This is important because it really does allow a far more scientific approach to depth control, and almost rules out the guess-work which is always part of fishing with a nylon leader.

It is essential to know how to tie the braid to the fly line; this is best done with a tubing.

ACCESSORIES

There are also various accessories which are extremely useful to have with you; these are given in no particular order of importance but simply as they spring to mind.

You will need something to make flies and/or the leader float: **Permaflote** is a favourite. On other occasions you will need something to make the fly and/or the leader sink, for which **zinc** is popular. It is also a good idea to have some **tung-sten putty**; try a piece on the leader next to the head of the fly for instant weight. And **condi-tioner** will help to make the line slick so that it glides easily through the rings.

There is also **Gehrke's Knot Perfect**, an amazing concoction, guaranteed to make all your knots smaller, stronger and quite non-slip; you can now trip knots as close as you like with total confidence. What Gehrke does is to eliminate as much as possible the heat generated when a knot is tied; the result is a perfectly compact and safe knot which is most unlikely to let you down at those crucial moments.

You might also consider some of the **strike indicators** that have inundated the market: simple pieces of plastic that stick on the leader, show up brightly and act in the same way as the coarse fisherman's float. They are light, highly visible and do not affect casting; but whether or not they are desirable is debatable. Geoff feels that they take away a great deal of the skill of detecting takes: after all, if we want fish that badly, we can always go out and buy them!

Even with **fly boxes** there is now a vast range, showing just how ingenious designers have become. You can now buy boxes that float, are waterproof, have moveable compartments, and really do everything bar choose the right fly for you! If you have selected your Sage rod and your Loop reel then you will probably go for the traditional aluminium fly box made by Wheatley; you might be tempted, whatever your budget, by one of the myriad patterns available.

Of course, you're not finished yet: you will also need **clippers** to finish off the knots, **priests** to finish off the fish, **magnifying lenses** and **hook-sharpeners** and **weighing scales** and virtually everything else you can think of.

Then there are **line-trays** if you do a lot of wading: look out for the line-tray made by the Creek Company, as this is very probably the best available. When not in use the soft frame means that it will fold flat against your body, held in place by a velcro tab.

You will certainly need **polaroid glasses**: a few years ago, most anglers realized that they needed polaroids – that was a step forward in

Christmas presents for ever more!

itself, although they thought that any brand would do. Then Optix came on to the scene with their glasses designed specially for anglers, and what a difference these made! The Optix Crylon standard frame, regular lens glasses are quite reasonably priced, but the range is vast and it pays to choose carefully.

When it comes to **fishing luggage** the new 'buzz' name on the market is Wychwood. The firm has really taken over the game market, just as it has coarse fishing luggage. But the great thing about Wychwood is that the business is run by anglers who know exactly what the practising fisherman wants. There are other, more traditional bags on the market, but Wychwood now has such a great range that everybody is catered for by them, and sales are reacting accordingly.

CLOTHING

We move to clothing; let's start at the feet first with the choice of waders.

Waders
Probably more questions are asked about waders than any other piece of fly fisherman's tackle;

Hats, waistcoats, waders – everything for the wet-weather fisherman.

here are some of the more typical ones, and their stock answers: felt soles are excellent if you are walking on rock or gravel. There they give plenty of grip, but if you need to walk up slippy slopes then they act as skis, and so are not to be recommended if you are fishing small natural baits. Cleated soles are perfect if you are wading on sandy bottoms or walking on muddy banks, but even they will slip on very slippery stones or rocks. They, therefore, might prove a problem if you are spending most of your time fishing in drizzle on reservoir walls.

The small tungsten studs of some soles give a good grip on slippery stones and work quite well on muddy banks. However, studded soles are not recommended in boats because they will scratch the bottom, and you will not be very popular if you ruin an expensive boat.

Waist-waders are a relatively new development and are becoming increasingly popular, for good reason: with waist-waders you can sit down without getting wet trousers; and you gain a significant advantage on thigh-waders when wading deeper water. Nor do they have any tendency to fall down, as do normal waders, and there are no shoulder straps to bother with.

The last question centres around the material waders are made of, especially with the appearance of neoprene into the market place. Neoprene is a high-quality material that offers exceptional warmth, and so is obviously very useful indeed when it comes to wading in cold water. The only problem is that neoprene is very expensive, and you will not get a good pair of neoprene waders for much less than a couple of hundred pounds. The other problem is that whilst neoprene waders are fine in cold weather and cold water, they are the very devil when things warm up; in fact I have seen people getting out of them and finding as much water inside as there is out! So think very carefully as to whether your budget and your fishing requirements are really that specialized.

Hats

Hats I always tend to ignore, although I am wrong to do so. The ultimate hat range comes from America: the wide 3in (8cm) brim provides shade and glare protection; the adjustable chin cord can be worn on windy days, and the high-tech sweat-band keeps the head dry and comfortable; there are ventilation eyelets, and the facility to move either or both sides of the brim away from the face by engaging the solid brass studs. All in all, a very strong, elegant and versatile piece of clothing. And if you are thinking about serious fishing in Scotland, Ireland or anywhere in the tundra belt, I would personally advise a Midge Net hat, guaranteed to exclude all midges and mosquitoes, no matter how small they are. It also features a clear vision panel which is very handy.

Waistcoats

Once again, the choice is absolutely enormous: you can buy waistcoats in varying lengths, materials and pocket numbers, so think very carefully before you make a purchase. I personally like the long Wychwood waistcoat, though the Bob Church moleskin does look rather elegant. There are even net waistcoats for very hot weather, as well as much shorter ones to be used when deep wading. If you are really serious about it you will probably end up buying two – though the problem then is always that what you really need when you are on the water is bound to be the waistcoat that is in the car!

Topcoats

Barbour has long held precedence in the market for topcoats, yet now new materials such as Goretex, Ventex and Aquatex are gradually taking over from the traditional wax cotton. This is largely because they are washable, they 'breathe' and they are completely waterproof. The choice is yours, and much depends on cost. Musto are very much the name of the future.

Safety

This is one area when cost should not be the first consideration. If you are thinking of doing any boat fishing at all, or any deep wading, then you really must consider some type of buoyancy aid. Did you know, for example, that in the last six years over 260 British anglers have drowned, and that this number increases every year? In fact more and more fisheries are now insisting that fishermen wear a safety device, and this is mandatory on some waters – and it makes sense to protect yourself sensibly. Remember there is a very important difference between lifejackets and buoyancy aids: lifejackets will turn you over and keep your head out of the water even if you are unconscious; buoyancy aids will simply provide assistance to a conscious person who can swim. You also have to decide whether to to invest in an automatic lifejacket or a manual one. The ultimate in safety is the Leeda Crewsaver automatic inflatable braces system: if you fall into the water conscious or unconscious the braces will automatically inflate, there is a large bladder-size in the model, and the increased buoyancy will ensure your head is out of the water all the time. This system is expensive but it really does work.

The critical measurement here is the number of Newtons buoyancy each garment offers. At around 100 Newtons you are talking of a buoyancy aid; you need at least 150 Newtons upwards to be talking of a lifejacket *per se*.

The Landing Net
We have one other important piece of tackle to discuss: the landing net to save the catch. Best sellers come from the Wilco Lux trout series, and the Trinet Trout or the Pelican Trout will probably be sufficient for most people most of the time, and not too expensive. However, the Whitlock nets must be the best: these nets are superbly engineered and extremely practical; moreover, their simple design is very pleasing to the eye, and they operate perfectly out of the water, being based on the Gye net principle of the net-head sliding along a shaft. They are probably the sort of net that the man with the Sage rod and the Loop reel would like to carry with him.

Of course, we're not finished even yet, and we could go on to talk about tippet dispensers, reel cases, glues, scissors and so on and so forth – but at least here you have a start, and most importantly something to work from. Confidence and a sense of purpose are badly needed when entering the tackle shop, especially for the first time.

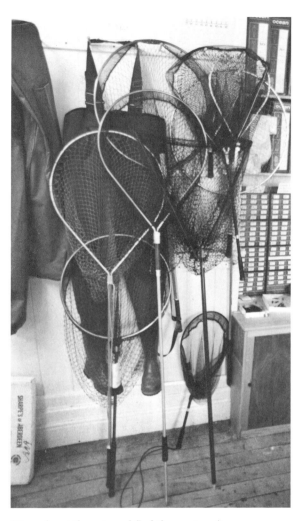

Never forget the net, and find the one to suit you.

CHOOSING FLIES

Once again, I must thank Geoff Franks of Sportfish for his advice regarding fly choice. Geoff is himself a very fine practising angler with a great deal of experience on many waters of all different sizes. In fact I did wonder whether to include the issue of fly tying in the book at all, because to do the subject justice you really have to go into great detail, besides which probably only about 5 per cent of the flies that are fished around the waters of Britain are in fact home tied, so the majority are

The choice of flies is never-ending.

bought, professionally tied ones. For those who wish to learn more about the art of fly tying, there are many instructional books available.

I must confess my own admiration for people who can identify a particular natural at the water, and then whip up an artificial in a matter of minutes that is so convincing it secures a limit bag before the sun has set! There is obviously something very rewarding and very elemental about such an ability, and I envy those who have it. Suffice it to say that I do not!

Buying Flies

Evidently there are two ways of buying flies. Firstly, there are anglers who try hard to be thoughtful, fishermen who have studied their home waters, believe they know what their trout are taking and consider fly fishing to be all about presenting an artificial as near as possible to the natural form. Of course, they may be wrong some or most of the time, but at least they are trying to

enter the world of the trout and offer an imitative pattern. Secondly, there are the anglers who regard fly selection rather like a sweet counter, a case of pick and mix; probably these are beginners wanting to hedge all possible bets, or who have picked up the latest magazines and seen what is currently in fashion – whether or not that fashion really suits their own particular fish.

Of course, there is nothing wrong with the second approach: everyone has to learn somewhere, and there are anglers quite happy just to throw out a large lure and whip it back all their angling lives. And who is to say that they do not have success and take their own particular pleasure from such a business? However, Geoff identified several fly types that every beginner (or international!) would be advised to have in his box.

Lures

All anglers, whatever their persuasion, should carry a stock of lures, in the principal colours of

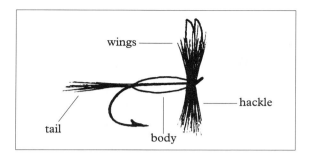

Fig. 9 *Lure.*

black, white, yellow and orange. There should be some leaded and some unleaded, with a selection of different sizes. There are days when a lure will work exceptionally well for no apparent reason.

Nymphs

All fishermen should then aim to build up a selection of at least the popular, well tried nymphs. Once more, these should vary in size and colour, with some leaded and some unleaded. There are stillwater trout experts who fish virtually all their lives with hardly anything but flies of the nymph form, and they are very successful anglers indeed.

Wet Flies

No angler can afford to ignore the traditional wet flies: these are patterns somewhere between the lure and the nymph, tied roughly to suggest an insect of some form or other, though the trout is not exactly sure which. This lack of precise identification on the part of the trout has not prevented it from falling to the traditional wet flies in vast numbers over many decades, so these should certainly be included in the box.

Dry Flies

Dry Flies have an important place in stillwater trout fishing, a fact until quite recently overlooked by many. Certainly during my stillwater fly fishing apprenticeship, dry flies tended to be considered the domain of the river fly fisherman – a sad error that blighted the efforts of many an angler. My own dry fly fishing experiences began on Derbyshire reservoirs back in 1961: my rod was a greenheart, and my reel, cadged, had come with line and a box of flies. Sadly the flies were all dries and the line was a sinker, so in my tenth year I spent three-quarters of my fishing time laboriously greasing a sinking line, desperate to make it float. Remarkably, I still caught quite a lot of trout, which does make you wonder whether a sub-surface line – as mine virtually was – was in fact something of a benefit...

Emergers

Another group of flies that should have a place in any angler's box are the emergers, flies tied to imitate insects that live in the water's film or actually on the surface. Watch the water surface on any warm, still summer's day and you will know exactly why you need these flies.

Terrestrials

At some time or another, most anglers will use the terrestrial type of fly: daddies, beetles, sedges, hawthorns, ants, and so on. Indeed, I myself find there is nothing more exciting than to watch daddy-longlegs being blown ashore by a reasonable breeze in the late summer, and the wild reaction of the trout which often sees my fingers fumbling with the knot!

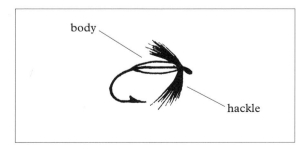

Fig. 10 *Wet fly.*

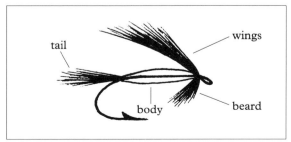

Fig. 11 *Dry fly.*

The great Dermot Wilson. He would rarely use lures, being a master of the dry fly.

Small Fish and Fry

This group consists of flies tied to imitate small fish and fry. One of the first of these to come to my own attention was the Polystickle, an artificial fly that emerged in my youth and reaped a good harvest once the trout were fly feeding in the margins. Obviously the distinction between this group and straightforward lures is somewhat blurred, but most anglers find it more gratifying to fish a lure with at least some pretension to imitation.

Gold Heads

The family of flies known as Gold Heads should also be considered an important category. Some outrageous claims have been made for the success of this comparatively recently introduced fly; for example, flies which are tied with a silver head are said to be successful because the head represents the air-sac of some insect... Well, such a claim is no doubt preposterous, but the simple fact is that Gold Heads work extraordinarily well for every conceivable type of game fish – quite why does not really matter, and I suspect most people have their own opinions.

Buy the Best

It is always advisable to buy the very best flies available; after all, they must be the most crucial part of the trout fisher's armoury. It's hard to tell a good fly simply by looking, of course, and you will need to use different companies' flies before you can come to any serious conclusions. Basically you want flies that behave well in the water, and which are tied in a durable fashion; you don't want a fly that looks awkward and comes apart at the second or third false cast! It is also vital to consider the hook type, and to buy flies that are tied to hooks with a good reputation: the last thing you want is a hook gape to straighten out when your best brownie is sliding towards the net. In fact the quality of the hook is nearly always represented in the price of the fly, so it is always worthwhile to pay a bit more.

In Conclusion

Fly choice is probably a fairly accurate reflection of human behaviour: thus there are those anglers on every bank who want to study their trout, to decipher at what depth and upon what their fish are feeding. On the other hand, there are those who are quite happy to whip a black lure through the water whatever the conditions, and attempt their four or eight fish limit as quickly as possible with the least possible mental exertion!

And finally, when the trout are going quite barmy and you can't raise a single fish, it is very often not the fly that is at fault but the fisherman. Probably half the time at least, the reason for failure is how the fly is fished, and not the actual pattern itself. Many anglers, and especially those relatively new to the game, would be far better off thinking about their fish and how their fly is presented, than rummaging furiously through an overloaded fly box looking for a magic solution.

A scene of contentment: the day's fishing done, the evening meal taken, and now sitting down to make some flies for tomorrow.

4 FLY FISHING TECHNIQUE

CASTING THE TROUT LINE

In my opinion too many people allow themselves to become unnecessarily worried about casting, the beginner because he is probably fearful that he is not doing it properly and so fails to obtain a great enough distance, thereby missing out on a fish, but even experienced anglers still seem to be convinced that somehow horizons have to be reached before the best fishing can be found. Obviously this is sometimes the case, but not generally, certainly in my experience.

The first prerequisite is to ensure that the rod and the line are matched, and are robust enough for the job you want them to do. Lines are important, so look after them: a line that is covered in sand, shingle or mud will not glide through the rings nearly as well as a line that is kept smooth. So, too, with the rings: check them frequently to ensure they are not becoming grooved, a situation which will ruin long or delicate casts.

Nearly all casting on stillwaters is done overhead with a to-and-fro motion. If there are obstructions behind the angler this does make for difficulties, but even so, very few trout anglers bother to spay or roll-cast. The general overhead cast depends on a number of things: first the speed of the line, which is obtained by moving the rod forwards and backwards, and gives real power and velocity. This is partly obtained by the leverage of the rod and the power of your wrist which produces a type of catapult effect. The speed that the line travels can be increased by pulling on the line above the reel and below the bottom ring, a method often called hauling. This downward pull simply increases the line speed and therefore adds distance.

The most frequent reason for failure is not maintaining the speed of the fly line, and one of the major faults is allowing the line to fall slack on its backward movement. The cast will certainly fall if it is not taut on the back-cast; it is as simple as that. Thus if you have twenty yards (18m) of line aerialized, the end of that line must travel the full twenty yards backwards beyond the rod tip; if

The man who has made fly casting into an art form: Hugh Falkus.

it travels only fifteen or so yards (13m) then there will be five yards (4m) slack in the line and the cast will fail. This really is important, and for this reason it is sometimes beneficial if the beginner especially looks at his back-cast as he is making it. This might seem ungainly, but at least he is assuring himself that the line is stretching out nicely behind him and that he is ready for the forward cast which will deliver the fly correctly.

The distance you can cast depends largely on the speed of the line but also on the air resistance that it meets, especially on the back-cast. Traditionally the angler is taught to stop the rod on the back-cast at the one o'clock point, and this is important: if this is done then the line travels back with a small loop and therefore very limited air resistance. It then straightens out nicely, goes taut and is ready to cast forwards. If, on the other hand, you allow the rod to dip back to the two o'clock position – or with some people, even the three o'clock – then the resultant loop is that much bigger and meets far more air resistance before it extends fully backwards. This, of course, slows down the whole velocity of the line and stops it extending nicely, tightly and quickly, and the cast is therefore all the more likely to fail.

The principle is the same with the forward cast, hence the importance again, of stopping the

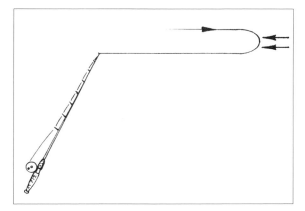

Fig. 12

Fig. 12 & 13 I am concentrating a great deal on the back cast because it seems to confound beginners more than anything else. The back cast presents all sorts of problems, not least of which is the ever-present threat of hanging up on bushes, trees or even long grasses. For this reason alone, it is a good idea for the beginner to look over his shoulder to see what the line is doing once it goes behind him. However, there are more important reasons. Figs 12–14 show how the back cast should proceed: the rod stops at around one o'clock on the clock face, and the line unfolds behind with a relatively small loop. You will notice that the air resistance on that loop is minimal. The line can then extend straight and high in the air before the forward cast commences (Fig. 13).

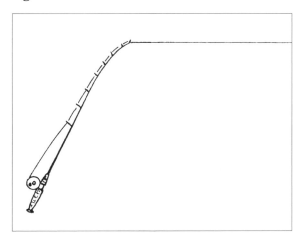

Fig. 13

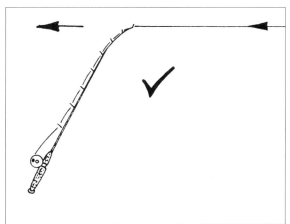

Fig. 14 How the back cast should extend: straight and true, and when it has reached this stage the forward cast can begin.

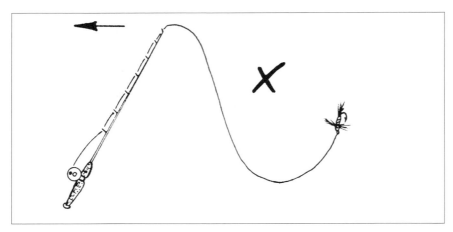

Fig. 15 *How the back cast should not proceed. Notice how the line begins to sag and to fall; it will be very difficult to generate enough power in the forward cast to throw the line out. It is also likely that the fly will catch grasses or shrubs behind.*

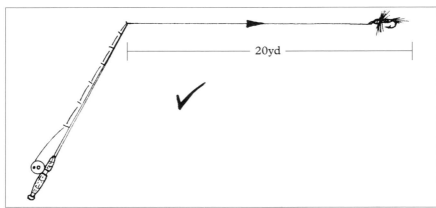

Fig. 16 *If you are aerializing 20yd (18m) of line then you want the fly to be 20yd (18m) from the rod tip. If it is only 15yd (13½m) from the rod tip then you have 5yd (4½m) of slack and the whole momentum of the cast is lost. If you wish, look over your shoulder at the beginning to see what your back cast is doing and you will soon see the mistakes.*

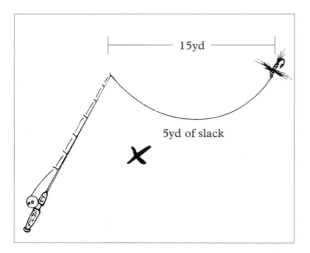

Fig. 17 *It is vital that no slack is allowed to form or the whole cast loses momentum.*

rod at eleven o'clock. That way the line travels forwards with a small loop which meets little air resistance before straightening out, ready to drop on the water. If you put the rod down to ten o'clock then the loop is much greater, it meets more air resistance and is therefore less likely to extend fully and fall straight onto the water – this is the way you get those horrible lapsed casts where the line just falls in great limp circles.

The basic principle is therefore to keep the rod working between the eleven o'clock and one o'clock positions – known as false casting – so that you can get more line out; this also helps dry the fly if you are fishing on the surface. This basic angle or arc can be altered a little – say, by thirty minutes each way – if there are obstructions that you need to clear such as a large bush behind you, or anything that will block the back-cast.

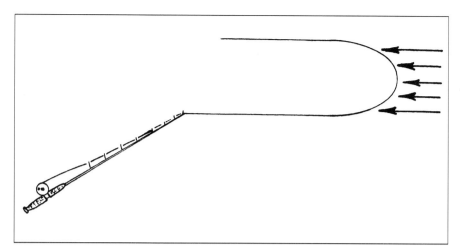

Fig. 18 A common mistake indeed! The rod tip has gone too far back, to two o'clock or even beyond, and the resulting loop in the fly line catches a great deal of air resistance and slows the whole cast down.

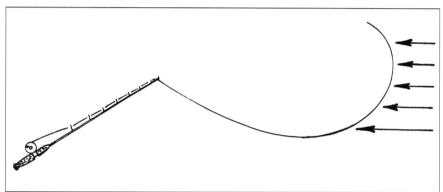

Fig. 19 This diagram shows how this cast will develop: soon you will find that the back cast simply collapses in a heap, seriously impeded by the air resistance and totally exhausted, without any momentum.

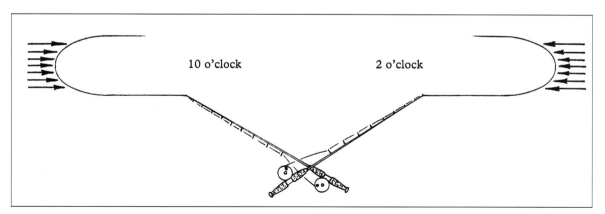

Fig. 20 (left) Again showing the problems caused by taking the rod tip too far back and creating extra air rationing.

Fig. 21 (right) This disastrous situation perpetuates itself: from two o'clock, the rod swings to ten o'clock on the forward cast and again the loop is too big and attracts too much air resistance for the line to shoot out properly. If the line does not collapse on the back cast then it will probably collapse in a heap on the forward cast. Always keep that loop small.

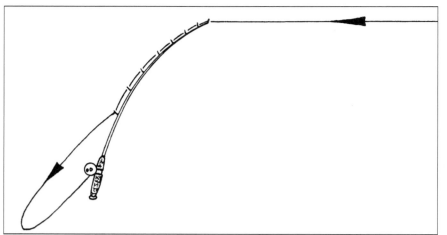

Fig. 22 *If you pull down on the fly line near the handle of the rod this will increase the speed of the line through the air – and casting, to an extent, is all about making sure that the line maintains its velocity. This is sometimes called 'hauling on the line', and you will find that it works well if there is a wind or for any other reason you find your line is not travelling at the required speed.*

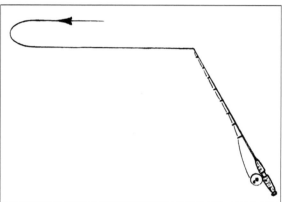

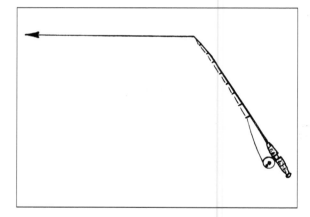

Fig. 23 *The forward cast, which can only be right when the back cast has been successful. Let me repeat, stop the rod at eleven o'clock so the line flies out swiftly and with a small loop, attracting minimum air resistance.*

Fig. 24 *With any luck and with a bit of practice the line will sing straight and true each time.*

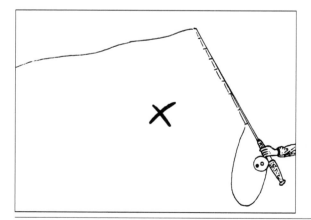

Fig. 25 *A frequent problem that beginners find with the forward cast. For some reason they tend to let go of the line with their fingers and this produces immediate slackness; once the tension is taken off, the possibility of the cast is lost and the line tends to fall in a snaking heap on the surface. It is vital to keep everything tight and working nicely. I have concentrated a great deal on the mechanics of the backward cast in particular, but it is also vital to remember that the tackle is important. Try to make sure as much as is possible that the fly line is free from sand or grit and as smooth as you can make it. Also check that your rod rings are not grooved, because this, too, will cut down the speed of the line and the distance that you can comfortably cast.*

Always remember to keep the line tight in your left hand as you are casting. If you let the line go slack for any reason then velocity and power are obviously lost and the whole cast will lose its momentum.

I have always believed that casting a fly is like riding a bicycle or swimming – is is a physical action that can only be learned by doing it. The whole process should be approached with confidence and enthusiasm, rather than diffidence and fear, and soon a nice, easy rhythm should be picked up. Overhead casting is not difficult and I have yet to find anybody who cannot cast with some degree of proficiency after a few hours. There is little mystique surrounding it, as there is with spay casting for instance, and in part at least this is because it is so simple! Keep that in mind, and if there are any problems try to work them out logically. Is your back-cast right? Are your loops tight? Is the line travelling with enough speed? Is the fly simply too heavy to cast suc-

cessfully? Are the rod and line matched? Are you trying to push a fly into too strong a wind? Are you being just a little bit too ambitious, making too many false casts and trying to aerialize just a few too many yards of line?

A last point about casting: a good trout fisherman always wears polaroid glasses because it does allow him to see under the surface in far greater detail. The number of times you will see a trout coming very close to you is great, and if you are alert to this you will be able to put a fly to it and possibly catch a trout in an area of water that you have not previously been fishing. And there is another reason for polaroids: safety. I have seen people with hooks caught very near their eyes, though thankfully never actually in one… yet. But this happens, and there are photographs in the angling press every year of the actual eyeball being hooked. Moreover, don't think it is only a head wind which will do this: in my experience some of the most dangerous winds

Watch out for the horse! I'm not joking! Horses, cows, and even worse, bulls, have all been caught on the back cast and mayhem ensues.

are those that whip in from either side of you and blow the fly off course when it is coming round again for the back-cast. If you find that your fly is hitting your shoulder, for example, when you are bringing it back out over the water, then it is wise to change your fishing position because very probably the wind is just too strong to continue fishing safely at that particular point.

Also, always make sure that the bank is clear behind you before attempting the back-cast: many of our best trout waters now have public access around the perimeter, and for every reason possible it is much better to hook a trout than a Sunday afternoon walker.

QUESTION OF THE LEADER

I remember happy days in the past when I was teaching in a boys' school: my friend, Chris, and I would take between ten and fifteen boys one evening a week on a trip to one of the local trout waters. Many of these boys went on to become very good fly fishers indeed, and Edgefield in particular was the perfect training ground because the trout were always on view and therefore enthusiasm remained high

In learning to fly fish I saw boys struggle for all sorts of reasons, and often for the more simple things such as casting technique or fly choice.

It is often possible to get away with a shorter leader when river fishing than it is on stillwaters.

But even the most unco-ordinated learned to cast a fly reasonably straight and over a fair distance within a day or two; and fly choice is generally made far too elaborate a consideration. Yet many boys persistently failed to catch fish. They were doing virtually everything right and yet coming away frustrated and fishless – and the whole daemon would be at fault, often a minor one, with the leader.

Leader Lessons at Edgefield

The leader is vital because it is the link between fly and fly line, the length of nylon that holds everything together, and either presents it all properly and effectively, or lands it all in a muddle so that it screams out a warning to every passing trout. There are several elements to bear in mind: first is the length of the leader itself.

It is very tempting for those who keep finding themselves tangled to allow the leader to become shorter and shorter, rather than going to the trouble and expense of tying on one of the right length. However, no matter what the depth flies are being worked at, once the leader becomes shorter than a certain length, then the fish will simply not respond. The critical limit varies from water to water, and depends on the conditions, and also on the wariness and intelligence of the trout in question. At Edgefield in those days that limit was between eight and nine feet (2½ to 2¾m) though I personally felt that a leader of eleven to twelve feet (3¼ to 3½m) was in actual fact a sensible minimum. Certainly I can rarely remember a trout being caught on a leader much less than nine or ten feet (2¾ or 3m) unless it was occasionally upon a lure thrashed back fast in the semi-darkness. Now, I know there will be exceptions to this rule, but I still maintain that if we are talking about the average water it is better to err on the long side rather than the short.

Leader thickness, especially at the fly, is also a crucial factor. I myself used to err too often on the light side, probably a result of my roach fishing background on the north-western canals where anything heavier than a cobweb spelt utter doom. Having said this, many aspiring anglers use leaders that are far too heavy. At Edgefield I found

A historic shot of one of fly fishing's heroes: the Rev. Alston, on one of his last trips to Ireland.

that any leader heavier than 4lb or so would almost certainly bring failure, unless a lure was being used and the light values were low. There were exceptions to this, but in general it was better to use a line between 3 and 4lb at the fly.

The next important issue concerns knots. If the knot that joins the fly line to the leader is untidy and bulky it will cause quite an obvious drag on the surface when the fly is being retrieved. Slightly less obvious are the knots on the leader itself, joining different strengths of nylon when a professional tapered leader cannot be afforded or is not wanted for some particular reason. At Edgefield these knots caused constant problems, for they did not allow the leader to travel through the water in the inconspicuous way required; a trimming of the knots very frequently resulted in a fish on the bank, much to the amazement of a boy who found it hard to

When trout like this are the quarry, you cannot afford to go too light with the leader.

believe that something apparently so insignificant could make such a vital contribution.

Pay attention to the state of the leader material itself: any kinks, loops or crinkles in it will prove disastrous. A leader must hang limp and straight and beautiful in order to be effective: it can never be if it is kinked here and there, and with angles as sharp as a dog's leg. Generally the reason can be traced back to a tangle, particularly if the fly has been caught up in a tree; even if everything has been retrieved apparently intact, the leader may well be significantly damaged. The rule established at Edgefield is still the golden one even today: change the leader after every tangle, and after every fish if the fight has been a difficult one. It is a rule that will always pay dividends.

Yet another problem is that monofilament flash gives off a definite signal which trout everywhere dislike. At Edgefield, some of the boys would rub their leaders in the damp clay that was found around the margins, and this worked to a great extent. However, whatever fly was being used, the leader also needed to be sunk into or slightly beneath the surface film at least near the fly. There are various leader-sink materials on the market nowadays and these work well, not only pulling the leader off the surface itself but also disguising that horrible glint that is so detrimental to success.

This fine trout was taken in a reasonable ripple so the leader could be relatively short.

In summary, the golden rules regarding leaders for all fly fisherman are these: use a reasonably long leader, of sensible diameter, with few and well trimmed knots, in good limp condition, rubbed not to glint and treated so as to sink. However, there are, of course, times when you have to think about the leader in more specialized ways.

Fishing the Hind's Pit on Exmoor

A few hour's fishing on the Hind's Pit will soon show how important the leader is. The Hind's Pit is not strictly a stillwater at all, but a large pool on the River Barle that in summer becomes almost without any current whatsoever; so it just about qualifies for the title. The trout resident in the Barle are only small, yet those of the Hind's Pit are often that little bit larger than the rest. I think this is probably because the pool is so difficult to fish that the trout here have longer lives than their brethren in the quicker water where presentation of a fly is easier. And, believe me, the Hind's brownies are exceptionally canny.

Also, these browns have not been stocked but are totally wild, and have had every opportunity to learn about food and the way it behaves, right from their fry stage. I believe this point is highly significant: because these trout have been able to watch natural food all their lives, as a result they are not so easily fooled as fish that have been recently introduced. So although these browns are only three, four or five to the pound, they exhibit more confidence in their environment than a recently stocked three-pounder.

The other thing to bear in mind is that in the summer when the river levels are low and the Hind's Pit is very still, the water is exceptionally clear. There are one or two runs that probably reach to five or six feet (1½ to 1¾m) at the most, but even here the grains of sand on the bottom, and the scale edges and fin rays of the fish are quite distinct.

All these factors, plus the absence of any current to give even a little life to the fly, make the Hind's Pit trout almost uncatchable. Now, I have become convinced that it is not the fly but the leader that is to blame. This I have proved at least to my own satisfaction, simply by hiding behind the oak tree on the steeper side of the pool and dapping a fly on the surface. It does not matter particularly what sort of fly is used, and you can dib it to send out rings – providing not an inch of leader lies on the surface, it will be taken by a miniature Barle brownie coming up like a rocket. However, let any nylon lie down on the water and you can twitch and flick the fly until nightfall and the trout will not take.

I began to think that this was the only way to catch the trout of Hind's Pit until the Exmoor rains fell and the water rose and clouded, and

When the water is as still as this, great care must be taken with the leader.

there was an appreciable current again. At these times, the little fish will make mistakes and be caught; but even so, the leader still has to be perfect, and if it isn't then your chance will be ruined even when visibility is down to a few inches.

However, after hours spent on Hind's Pit I have found just small things that can be done to disguise the leader problem. For example, when fishing a weighted nymph, if you can see any bottom weed, try and get the nylon to lie right down in it – then a take is possible. This type of presentation is extremely difficult, however, and I have only managed it where the water has been two or three feet (¾ to 1m) deep and relatively close in. For most purposes the technique is not really a viable one.

I've also tried using a dry fly with a leaf or a twig on the leader pushed hard up against it: this often works. Obviously the trout sees only the fly and the leaf, and has no inkling that the leader is present at all: a cheat perhaps, but it works! You can also place the leader to lie over any rubbish that is on the water surface, to disguise it as best you can. Often, of course, there is not sufficient flotsam available, and the method falls down; but after a wind, when twigs and leaves have been blown from the branches or flowers from the banks then it is a method that can occasionally work.

Difficult Trout at Coldingham Loch

At least when I knew it years ago, Coldingham Loch was a real gem of a water quite near the River Tweed. When things were dour on the Tweed and the salmon were not running, I would drive north and fish for these difficult trout in an often difficult water. The loch itself seems to teeter on a cliff with the sea almost within casting distance, and it is this geographical position that makes the water exceptionally deep and clear.

It was often my experience there to find the fish deep, between ten and fifteen feet (3 and 4½m) at least. The technique I began with at Coldingham was always sunken lines, but I never found these particularly successful: with a sinking line you have to work the fly with at least some speed to prevent the line dragging it into bottom weed. The problem was that a fast retrieve with a small nymph

and imitators was frequently not what the trout wanted; what it would respond to was a very slow retrieve. In fact sometimes it seemed better to let the fly hardly move at all; and for that you obviously needed a floating line and a very, very long leader, certainly twenty feet (6m) or more.

Casting such a leader is not the problem you might imagine, as long as the weather is not totally behind you. In fact with just a little breeze behind, you can put out a fly a long way. The fly has to be leaded if it is to sink decently and at a steady, predictable rate. The weight of this fly will turn the leader over even a long one, if a wind is not head-on.

These long leaders work well at Coldingham, and equally well on every deep water I have tried since the actual technique of casting them was learned, naturally enough, from Brian Clarke:

> First of all, pull a few yards of line off the reel and allow them to fall at your feet. Next, pull a couple of yards of fly line (to which the long leader is attached) through the top ring. Now, grasp the weighted fly in the left hand (you will need a little lead in it to carry the leader down to the bottom in deep water) and trapping with the other hand the line against the butt, slowly aerialize in front of you the large loop consisting of the long leader and the two yards of fly line by wafting the rod gently from side to side. Once the loop between your left hand, holding the fly, and the rod tip is airborne, gradually allow the weight of the line in the air to pull more and more line from the coils on the ground by releasing the pressure of the fingers which held it jammed against the rod handle. As you do this, and continue wafting the rod end, the length of line in the aerialized loop will, of course, get longer and longer and exert more of a pull on the top of the rod. When you judge that there is enough line in the air to flex the rod, simply release the fly from the left hand and go into a normal casting rhythm.

Clarke goes on to denigrate his succinct and brilliant description of the long leader cast as being fiddly and complex: in fact, providing his instructions are carried out stage by stage, you will find the cast quite easy and swift to make, and not at all off-putting.

Indicators

I have always dismissed indicators as making fishing rather too easy, and have regarded sensing the take as one of the great skills; it is a facet of trout fishing that I have worked on throughout my own career. However, convictions sometimes change, and quite a few incidents have occurred to make me reconsider to some extent.

In August 1994 I accompanied a journalist on a very rough and ready journey to the borders of Siberia and Mongolia; the quarry was taimen, the great Asian landlocked salmon. However, these were rather noticeable by their absence, and because food ran very short we were obliged to fish in order to eat. Now, one of the more sizeable fish in these desolate regions is the lenok trout; this is very much like our own Western trout but with a slightly barbel-like mouth, an adaptation to enable it to feed on algae and the like as well as insects, as these are in short supply after a mid-summer burst.

The rivers were very low, and in many instances we were fishing big, still pools some 50 or 60yd (45 to 55m) long and anything up to 10ft (3m) deep. There was no flow whatsoever – or at least none noticeable – and so we were really still-water fishing for the lenok, and takes were very difficult to see. This was undoubtedly because they insisted on small flies worked very slowly which they took in the most imperceptible of fashions. In fact I was beginning to tear my hair out, not simply at the thought of missed sport but rather because we were all starving!

Then Georg Schu arrived with his indicators. Georg is a restauranteur from Germany, very keen indeed on his fly fishing, and who possessed every last little bit of tackle – including a bright orange indicator.

I watched with great interest. To ensure that I registered any takes I was receiving, I was being obliged to fish small nymphs rather faster than I wanted; Georg could, on the other hand, really inch his about and be totally confident that the indicator would tell him when a lenok had struck. On the whole, over a few days' fishing, I was left in no doubt that the indicator did give Georg something of an advantage, and at last I began to use

one myself. Let me tell you, in this sort of terrain, the niceties of sport fishing are not in any way as important as the necessity of living, and if indicators made the chances of our getting out alive more likely, then indicators it would be! All in all, it was quite an experience to find myself fishing to live, and one that in the end I really savoured. Somehow it made deep sense of all the trout fishing I had done in the past, and what was interesting was the fact that the locals, trying to catch food with nets, faired much less well than we did. Without our artificial flies I don't think we would have ever lived to see the helicopter return.

On my return to England I visited a new water, a relatively small pit with plentiful rainbow trout, being fished by 'Robbie' Robins and his wife Audrey. I was immediately struck by the fact that they were both using indicators – after years of ignoring these things they now seemed to be everywhere I looked. There was no doubt, talking to Robbie, that he was a supporter of indicators, and he gave the following reasons: first, they indicate far better than anything the leader or even the fly line can do. Second, they allow you to fish a fly absolutely accurately at whatever depth you want. Before indicators, I suppose we all had some idea at what depth our flies were fishing, but I am sure we would often be out by quite a few feet one way or another. And the third advantage of indicators was apparent in the way that Robbie was actually fishing: he was casting some way from the bank and letting the line and flies drift around in a slow arc. The indicator rode the surface exactly like a mini-float would do in coarse fishing, and assisted the smooth successful drift that he was fishing. There was something of a chop on the water and the indicator was certainly out twenty-five yards (22m); at that sort of range I seriously doubt whether anybody in those conditions would have seen a gentle take at all, and Robbie left me in no doubt that indicators obviously have some place.

In December I was offered a most excellent day's fishing on the River Dove by Tony Bridgett. Now, this was prime grayling water, and I was at first somewhat surprised to see Tony setting up our gear in the car park complete with a small

An indicator on the line can certainly help when the angler is not too experienced or the trout are very shy-biting.

home-made indicator on each of our lines. These were very small balsa-wood affairs with a hole bored in the middle and painted orange. They were simply fixed on the line in the same way as any coarse fisherman's float but by the novel technique of a thorn broken from the hedgerow. We wandered up the freezing valley and Tony began with the first small pool. Rather like Robbie, he simply cast a gold-headed nymph out into the current and let it work this way and that, exploring all the water under the small indicator.

As the day progressed, it was quite apparent that this was the most effective way of fishing with the nymph for grayling I personally had ever come across. I just could not believe the ferocity of the takes. One minute a small orange blob was bobbing merrily about on the slate-grey surface of the Dove, and the next it would be slashing six or seven inches under the surface, heading upstream in no uncertain fashion at all. I'm not saying it was impossible to miss takes because I certainly did, but there was no doubt that I saw every grayling offer that day, which generally is something I rarely feel confident about at all. So, indicator strikes again!

I suppose the nearest I have come to using indicators in the past is the old and tried technique of simply tying a dry fly onto the line above the nymph and using that as a float – with the added advantage that it is sometimes, occasionally, taken itself. However, there are all manner of disadvantages with the dry fly, not least the fact that it often begins to sink of its own accord, pulled under by the weight of the waves and the weight of the nymph. With the indicator there is none of this problem. I tried five or six different types of indicator, and although I don't think any of them beat Tony's home-made example, they would all, obviously, do the job exceptionally well. My own personal favourite would probably be the Float-Do, a re-usable, pliable floating putty bite indicator that can be moulded to any shape you want and is simply pressed onto the line. Like all the other indicators, it is available in a range of colours for utmost visibility. I like to think the DO gives just that little bit of flexibility so that you can fish whatever shape or size you want according to the conditions.

I still don't know: without indicators, after all, I might not be here, but since it is unlikely that my life will depend on a brown trout in the future, I am still not a whole-hearted supporter of indicators. I still at least half think that proper study of the leader and its movements is the way to become a better-than-average stillwater fisherman.

5 THE EDGEFIELD EXPERIENCE

EARLY EDGEFIELD DAYS

It took me a little while to identify the spark that ignited the renaissance of my affair with stillwater trout fishing: the decline in East Anglia's roach had persuaded me to start looking for pastures new, but there was something else, too. Perhaps part of it was the sight of the old greenheart rod that I had used as a child back in Tintwhistle days that hung in pride of place in the hallway of my house, serving as a constant reminder of glorious days gone by. But there was yet another stimulus, looking back I realized that it was an otter!

I had lived on the north Norfolk coast for a long while, and had become fascinated with the River Glaven, a small, beautiful, meandering stream that runs into the North Sea at Cley. Its fish beguiled me, but so did the constant movement

A shot of the north Norfolk coast in the distance and a fine old estate lake – one holding trout – in the foreground. This was a geographical area that fascinated me.

of otters in the valley, and in about 1977 I began to track these elusive and captivating creatures for myself.

In studying the Glaven otters I accumulated a deep knowledge of the valley and all the streams and pools that fed it. It was, and still is today, an enchanted area very little spoiled, in part because of the invincibility of the large landed estates in which the bulk of the valley lies. In fact there is an air of immortality over the whole area, and this has served nature well; at that time it certainly benefited the otters which I began to see more and more frequently. Thus I came to know every inch of that exceptional watershed, until finally one evening I found myself staring at Edgefield Lake. It was June, and the weather was quite golden. The setting sun was glinting off the water and insects were rising to the steady flop of the trout. There was just one man on the water and as I watched, twice his rod moved, his reel sank and two fine rainbows prepared to make their way to his kitchen. It was a wonderful scene, and I wandered off down the valley thinking hard about what I had been missing those past years.

The very next day I rooted out what fly tackle I still possessed, made good the glaring deficiencies by a single visit to a Norwich tackle shop, and that evening went and knocked on the door of Edgefield Hall to ask for an evening ticket. The Hall itself was enough to captivate me: it was Tudor, imposing and full of mystery, and when its owner appeared, the Edgefield spell was complete.

Gerry Gent was a man with vision. He had cleared out the original, silted up lake below the Hall and had refilled it with fresh, sparkling water and these leaping trout that I saw everywhere before me.

This visit inaugurated a fabulous time, and goodness knows how many day tickets I bought from Gerry over the next few seasons, never regretting a single penny. I would try to go three or four times a week, beginning on the water as early as April and fishing right on into October, even until the lake was sometimes fringed by ice. The times spent there were always magic, whatever the time of year or weather that raged... and anyway, in my recollection the sun always shone.

Edgefield Lake itself was around four acres, perhaps five if you included the large feeder stream – the upper Glaven in fact – that ran into it and which trout frequently explored. Its shape was typical of an estate lake, roughly triangular with a dam wall at the far end where the water was deepest. Gerry had also made sure that the banks were not totally regular, and here and there had bays and islands constructed, thus breaking up the formal shape of the original lake.

Depths were also typical of the average estate lake, with the deepest water to be found running like a spine down the middle, following the course of the old Glaven bed. At its deepest point, Edgefield Lake probably reached 8 or 9ft (2½ to 2¾m), but the average was much less than this and in some of the bays you were lucky to find just 18in (½m) of water. None of this really mattered too much to the trout because the water was sparkling fresh, introduced daily by the ever-bubbling Glaven. Even at the very height of summer when the rest of the land was parched with drought, Edgefield Lake never suffered and its water was always clear and cool, straight from the springs and streams of the surrounding downs.

Weed could grow profusely at times, which was bad from the angler's point of view but beneficial to the fish. In fact, Edgefield was an incredibly rich lake, partly because of the water and partly because reclamation had created such a dynamic, exploding environment. Natural food proliferated, and some of the evening hatches were extraordinary to witness. The trout that Gerry Gent introduced therefore waxed fat, particularly as they were fine fish in the first place. Most were rainbows but about 30 per cent were browns, some quite large fish of over 2lb, although these quickly made 3lb and more.

In the early days I was a daemon with the Baby Doll, and for most trips it was the only fly I used. Sometimes I fished them large, sometimes small, in green and yellow but generally white, and did quite well with them – though this could be attributed to the amount of effort I put in and the number of fish I covered in the course of a day's fishing. In those days I was very much influenced by a certain individual we called 'the Tax

Early days at Edgefield: camouflage is important.

Collector': this gentleman was ferocious – he appeared early every Sunday so that he could stake his place on the Point, a strip of land running out into the lake which commanded several prime areas. The Point belonged to the Tax Collector on a Sunday, and woe betide any stranger who should blunder his way in there first!

The Tax Collector would pay his money – a mere £6 in those days – and make his way to the Point, where he was evidently determined that every penny would be well spent. He flogged the hours away, casting like a robot, always with lures which he dragged at a set speed back through the water. He didn't fish all the time; at 11.00am he had a fifteen-minute break, and at 1.00pm he had lunch for exactly half an hour. At 4.00pm he rested again, for fifteen minutes, to consume his last sandwich and the dregs of the flask.

I was in considerable awe of the Tax Collector: he always caught his limit, always looked self-assured and never asked for advice. In those early days he seemed the complete fisherman and I felt he quite overshadowed my efforts. However, things were to change.

EDGEFIELD DISCOVERIES

I suppose there was nothing wrong with my Baby Doll days because I was catching fish and I was enjoying myself; but increasingly it bothered me that I didn't know why I was catching those trout – they simply came along at random. I do remember making tentative theories: for example I often noticed that a change of colour or size would bring an instant response; perhaps only one fish, but enough to lift my spirits and make me flog the water even harder. I also noticed that if I moved round the lake results were better than if I spent too long in one particular position; even the Tax Collector used to work his casts around in wide arcs rather than concentrate on one particular

I began to realize that concealment was essential.

spot. And sometimes it paid to work the lure deep, at others much nearer the surface. Varying the rate of the retrieve had some effect, too. In short, I was beginning to impose some sort of rationale onto the method. It was satisfying, but only to a point, and I didn't know how to progress.

There was at Edgefield a certain individual whom I shall call the Silent Man, an angler I'd been aware of for many trips but had never made any contact with. He kept himself remote and perhaps I found him intimidating, but I think all of us were intrigued by his style of fishing. He did not flog the water, and hardly seemed to catch much at all; though when he did cast, he generally caught a fish. Often he would leave, his limit bag completed, long before the Tax Collector had even landed a fish. Finally, I made up my mind to approach him.

He listened to me without making much response, then arranged to meet me again at the weekend. When we did, he produced a book: *The Pursuit of Stillwater Trout* by Brian Clarke. This book revolutionized my attitude to stillwater trouting; without its inspired teaching I would simply have become bored by my repeated lack of success. I read it avidly and found that it preached the most exciting doctrine: that real success and satisfaction with stillwater trout can be achieved through intellectual effort, through reading the water, through thinking about trout in a truly three-dimensional way. For those of us chained to long-distance casting and Baby Doll stripping this was the breakthrough that we needed: stillwater trouting suddenly became magic in my eyes.

I met the Silent Man five days later and gushed out my excitement over Clarke's book. He listened, and obviously realized that I was ready to be taught higher skills. The first thing he impressed on me was how important it was to try and decipher the water in all its different moods; it was not enough just to settle for one of the few well trodden favourite spots around the lake where I could put in a reasonably long line without fear of tangles. I was taught that above all it was essential to take my time. He showed me a hill above the lake, and told me to sit and watch the water for five or ten minutes before going down to the bankside. The purpose of this was to sink oneself into the rhythms of the natural world, to study oneself and to wash away the humdrum cares of everyday human life. It had a more practical side, too: during this period of calm and thought it was important to study the wind direction and its force, to watch where any ripple might be scudding the surface, to note any re-occurring rises, any new weed crops, or anything that might affect the fish or the fishing to come. After a few minutes I realized that it was true, and that you could approach the water in a totally different frame of mind: I found that I was more relaxed, more 'in tune', and ready to start fishing in a more rational frame of mind.

The Silent Man always liked to watch his fish, and for this reason avoided any water where the clarity was not near perfect. Soon this was an attitude I began to adopt myself, and to this end bought some polaroid glasses; a pair of the best quality glasses is the most useful accessory any stillwater trout fisherman can buy. I also realized that stealth along the bankside was important. At first I thought this was strange, especially when 95 per cent of the other anglers on the water would be marching around as if they were on some sort of victory parade. However, now I had been taught differently and so I would creep in and hide, bending low behind rushes and melting behind tree trunks, and although some mocked, my catches undoubtedly rose.

Moreover I took to wearing drab, inconspicuous clothes, and most especially a hat with a good brim that the Silent Man assured me would cover a good deal of my forehead, an area that will too readily catch the sun and flash a telltale gleam of light to the fish. I realized increasingly how alarming the flash of a pale face is to trout; they

Edgefield trout had tails like shovels.

might well be used to such sights, but even so I was beginning to appreciate that such things put them on the alert, making them wary of anything out of the ordinary, and so much less likely to feed. This was one of the important things that I learnt, and something that has been confirmed time and again over years of fishing: camouflage, stealth and slow movements are all essential.

So the Silent Man's instruction continued: he told me to look first for areas of calm, and to begin any approach to Edgefield in these places. This seemed strange to me initially because I knew that on larger waters anglers looked for areas of ripple where there was more chance of oxygenated water, food and therefore active trout. But the Silent Man explained: with polaroids on, it was a more realistic to watch for specific, individual fish and to try to catch those. This became the hallmark of my new approach: no longer was it enough to whip the water indiscriminately, waiting for any young stocky to wander along. Now, I copied the Silent Man in attempting to land not just a limit bag, but four fish of above-average size and in the peak of condition; and to do this I needed to select my fish.

So that was the first step, to try those areas of calm water where it was possible to study the water beneath the surface, to pick out fish and to go after them individually. Wind direction was crucial in deciding which bay or tree-lined piece of bank I would make for, and then very often I would experience some of the most exciting still-water fishing there is: the stalking of identified, above-average fish. Between them Brian Clarke and the Silent Man had taught me a great deal, and Edgefield began to unfold its charms in ways I had never dreamed of before.

EDGEFIELD STRATEGIES

I soon developed a profound and long-lasting respect for rainbow trout, even stockies. I had only just begun my association with the Silent Man when I found myself pretty well alone one afternoon on the water. Gerry Gent came over for a brief conversation before moving down to the stewponds and bringing back with him a hundred or so trout; these he put into the lake at various points, six or seven fish at a time. One small shoal he put in immediately to my left. Five fish moved steadily out into the lake, exploring their new-found freedom, but one, a stocky that was really a most unremarkable fish, stayed in the bay where I was fishing and for some reason I decided I would try to catch it. I put a small nymph, a size 16 Pheasant Tail, right in front of its nose and the reaction was immediate, its mouth opening round the fly. I struck, but found I was too early: the trout merely keeled over, wriggled for perhaps two seconds and then was free. I did not curse my luck greatly because I realized I could probably catch a better specimen in its place, so I continued my pursuit of a decent looking fish of about 1½lb.

Pursuing the Scar-backed Stockie

The story does not end there: in fact it did not end for the next three months. Every time that I visited Edgefield I would look into that bay and see the same stocked rainbow trout that I had pricked so momentarily. The fish was quite easily identifiable by a rather large cut on its back which had healed unglamorously. Over and over, day after day, that fish was pursued by the never-ending stream of day-ticket anglers. Fly after fly it saw whipped past its nose, and yet it continued to survive. I became more and more interested with this fish, and soon began to pursue it quite purposefully myself. It was a fascinating experience: I could persuade it quite easily to look at a fly, and even to follow it only inches behind; but to get it actually to make a mouth at an artificial, and to hook it fair and square, was beyond me. I could hardly believe it. I told the Silent Man of my problems, and he laughed and told me it should be an object lesson never to take even the humblest stocked rainbow trout for granted. And he was right.

I lost count of the fruitless hours I put in after that fish, and for three months it went uncaught – until, finally, it disappeared. I made what enquiries I could and came to the conclusion it had not actually been caught by an angler;

*All tackled up, and raring to go! A real excitement runs through the angler at this stage –
but it's advisable to stop and study the water first.*

perhaps it had slipped off deeper into the lake, or
been taken by a pike or one of my otters passing
in the night. All I can safely say is that it wasn't
me that put an end to that stocked rainbow trout:
it was way beyond me in cunning, even though its
only knowledge of a hook had been for a mere
two seconds.

Understanding Trout Behaviour

As the weeks progressed, I became more and more
like the Silent Man himself, spending far more
time watching trout than actually trying to catch
them. However, I was beginning to appreciate that
it all paid off in the end, and that it was better to
watch a good fish for an hour and a half and catch
him within five minutes that to flog mindlessly for
two hours for either nothing at all or for a below-
average fish. These hours I spent looking into the
aquarium-like water at Edgefield taught me a great

deal about the trout's body language, something I
found just as fascinating as fishing itself.

I began to recognize when trout were listless and
lethargic, with no interest in feeding or life itself; I
suppose in our terms those fish were really fast
asleep. In this mode they seemed to lie close to the
bottom, or certainly beneath mid-water, hardly
moving at all except perhaps to flick a fin every
now and again to maintain position. Like this the
eye moves little, and the gills only work enough to
pass oxygen; the white of the mouth, for example,
rarely if ever shows. Such trout are not easy to
scare: over and over I watched anglers come past,
just five yards (4½m) away, shouting or chattering
or waving their rods, and there would be no reaction. Needless to say, when a trout was like this it
was futile to put a fly to it; you could work whatever you wanted within inches of its nose and eli-
cit not the tiniest response.

When such a fish begins to wake again the signs are obvious: fin movement definitely increases and the body begins to flex as well; the gills work more energetically, and from time to time the eyes roll. Eventually the tail fin kicks in and the trout starts to move consciously through the water. This is a good sign: feeding is about to start.

The trout on the prowl became unmistakable to me. There was something alert about it, every fin was erect, taut and quivering, and the dorsal fin would be held particularly high. The fish would almost certainly follow some sort of patrol route, but – and this is important – it would dart off it frequently, to the left or right to investigate any apparent food source. This would be an eminently catchable rainbow or brown trout.

I also witnessed all manner of feeding behaviour apart from the traditional surface rise. In fact at Edgefield I began to realize that about 95 per cent of feeding took place a long way beneath the surface, and that it was comparatively rare to see a

fish actually show at all. I was also surprised at how frequently trout buried their heads into mud, or weed, or under stones, rooting aggressively for food in the way of a carp, tench or bream. Admittedly a great deal of the trout's feeding was done artistically, picking off a food item here or there as it emerged from cover; but the normal trout is obviously quite willing to get its hands dirty, as it were, in order to secure a good meal. Indeed, when I saw a trout feeding energetically in and around the bottom I came to feel sure that a well presented, heavily weighted nymph would almost certainly do the business, as they say, and time and again I was proved correct.

The Taking Fish

A take on the Baby Doll was undoubtedly exciting: the line would suddenly become alive and the rod hoop over, an electric feeling in itself. However, this was nothing to the excitement of a witnessed take, especially after two or three hours

The browns were big and beautiful, and I would do anything to catch them.

had been spent after a particular fish. Sometimes at Edgefield it was possible to see the mouth open or the nymph or imitative fly disappear; at other times one had to fish on a hunch and recognize what a taking fish actually looked like. I began to know exactly when a trout had engulfed a piece of food, simply from the flash of white of its mouth and the chop of the jaws and often the rapid eye movement. Also the body often quivered as – presumably – the adrenalin pulsed through it. If my fly were in the immediate vicinity when I witnessed such a thing, I would then tighten, and more often than not be proved a correct and successful fisherman.

Sometimes the Silent Man would watch me, perhaps for two or three hours at a time; he would say nothing until the end, and then he would run through my catalogue of errors, occasionally praising me for something I had done correctly. Little by little as the months progressed his visits at my shoulder became shorter, and my catalogue of errors also began to diminish. Finally the time came when he was content merely to wave a greeting, and occasionally call out some piece of advice over the water.

One of these pieces of advice regarded the ripple. Inevitably, there were times when fishing the

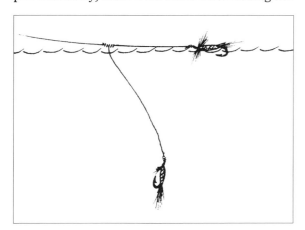

Fig. 26 *A dry fly can be very useful when it comes to drifting a nymph just sub-surface. It will stop the nymph sinking too far beneath the surface and it will also act as a bite indicator, slashing under the surface if a trout takes the nymph. The added bonus is that it is an indicator which trout will frequently try to eat!*

calm area simply did not produce: perhaps some people had been there immediately before my arrival and fished it hard, and either caught in it or driven away all the fish that had been using it. Or again, in very hot weather there would be times when the fish were simply too lethargic to do much at all in shallow, unruffled water. Although the odd fish could be tempted in weather like this, it was obvious – in high summer especially – that some lively water would be needed, even considering that Edgefield was largely fed by cool spring water. Then it would be a case of fishing any pieces of ripple around the lake.

The Silent Man often took a thermometer with him, and he would show me just how the slightest breeze – especially coming in from the coast half a dozen miles away – would lower the temperature of the surface layer by just a degree or two. This might not be much, but it was enough to encourage trout to move and to feed, and all one had to do was to cast a line out with the fly fished just sub-surface and let it drift before the breeze; like this, takes would be steady and confident. However it was exciting to see the line pulled tight against the drift, it was not the style of fishing I enjoyed; I found it impersonal after stalking the bays, and of course it was almost impossible to select the better-than-average type of fish that I was now wanting.

Catching the Big Brownie

Under the Silent Man's tuition I was also beginning to take a much more active interest in browns. These were rarely caught, and indeed Gerry was putting in a smaller and smaller percentage because of this. Most anglers preferred rainbows because they were more lively; but that very fact made the browns soon become the more desirable of the two strains to me.

I soon discovered that the browns liked to patrol the deepest water along the dam or down the central channel – not all the time of course, but for a noticeable period of their lives, and especially in the full daylight hours. Fishing the dam was not always easy because it seemed to attract anglers like a magnet, but here and there the central channel was accessible to the bank fisherman, and there were two points in particular where the lake sides narrow together and a relatively short cast would see you fishing in the deepest water.

In hot weather especially, when the rest of the lake was comatose, that was an area I would make for, and fish with the long leaders that Brian Clarke had recommended. Sometimes these leaders seemed extravagantly long, even 22 or 23 feet (6½ to 7m) that took some casting, especially with the heavily leaded nymph that was vital to this method. The idea would be that I would put out a reasonably long line, let the nymph sink right to the bottom zone and then inch it back. And I mean *inch*: a single cast might take three or four minutes to work through, and I liked to imagine my fly searching every single crevice and looking like any other small, dark twitching food item.

I rarely lost patience with this type of fishing and went to great lengths to visualize my fly down there, doing everything to try and work it just a little bit more imaginatively. Sometimes Nigel, Gerry Gent's son, would come and sit by me and talk to me about all manner of things; but still my concentration never wavered. You see, the take could come out of nowhere, and frequently did. It was not unusual to have been fishing for two or even three hours in this way when suddenly the line would pull tight – not violently, but just steadily and surely, and a big brown would be on, deep down in the cooler water.

Often when sitting on the hill I would notice that a slight breeze was blowing up all the surface refuse, and rubbing into various pockets around the water. Not all this would be edible, and much was bankside clutter or plumage from water birds; there were dead insects here and there, and often other live ones would get trapped in the layer of scum that gradually built up. These areas did not produce many fish, but they frequently attracted the better-than-average specimens. It was as though the older fish had learnt that these slicks that began to appear by the late afternoon held rich pickings for them. Often the behaviour of fish in these areas was very subtle, and you really needed to study the surface to see anything much at all.

It was on just such an occasion that I took my biggest brown from the water. It was July, early afternoon, and a storm was building steadily away to the south, approaching quite rapidly. The day had been very still and hot, and I found a bay towards the head of the lake which was thickly covered with struggling insects amongst the usual feathers, pieces of reed and other rubbish. Fortunately the bay was surrounded by quite high weed growth which gave me fine cover, and I was in there for at least half an hour before I saw a fish that really excited me. It was a brown that I put at about 4lb, and very slowly and delicately it was working through the scum, occasionally pushing its neb through to suck down some insect.

I watched the fish for around twenty or thirty minutes, noticing that it had a very definite route which took about ten minutes to complete. It was all made more dramatic as the sky continually darkened and the once distant rumble of thunder grew noticeably closer.

Finally, when I was quite confident of the trout and my strategy, I tied on a large dry fly dressed on a size 12 hook: it was an old Mayfly pattern that I had in my box, and I felt that it would do the trick as the fish was feeding on nothing specific. I did not prepare the fly in any way to float proud, but simply cast it into the scum a minute or two after the trout had passed that particular point. I even pulled the fly a little under the surface so that it would lie half in, half out of the water in a way typical of the real thing. Seven or eight minutes passed and the lightning was now dancing along the valley when the big brown made its way back into my vision, towards the zone of the fly.

Would it see it? I began to jig the rod tip just a small amount, but enough to transmit down the line to the fly and make it send out little rings of distress. That big brown never hesitated, but came to my fly and took it with a slow and confident gurgle that I could hear roll across louder than the storm itself. Not a particularly skillful capture, but rather I saw it as a reward for understanding the water – and at last I had caught a brown approaching the lost Tintwhistle monster years before.

A real mixed bag: an old painting that reminded me so much of Edgefield. There, pike could be a problem, and there was always a chance of a carp getting in from the up-valley lake.

The Giant Rainbow

One fortunate day I was in the southern corner of the dam, hiding behind my usual willow tree, when some 10yd (9m) out I saw a particularly large gleam. I couldn't be sure, but I had the feeling this was a very big trout indeed. I continued to watch for a good forty-five minutes, and a picture of what was happening began to form in my mind. Some ten yards out, a bank of thick weed grew up from the bottom in about four or five feet (1 to 1½m) of water, and I became more and more convinced that a large trout had adopted that weed-fringe as his patrol route. Half-a-dozen times I saw that gleam, almost certainly made by a fish turning to intercept an insect.

I guessed the trout was swimming about three feet (1m) beneath the surface and a couple of feet (½m) away from the thick weed behind it, so I knew it would need a heavily weighted fly to land on the surface, just on the lip of the weed and then to sink quickly to the required depth: a well-leaded Olive nymph tied to a size 14 I felt would do the trick. It was my habit to fish quite light at Edgefield, but I wasn't sure with this creature, and so I stepped up from my normal 3lb bottom to 5lb, and waited until the fish gleamed again.

I'd practised my cast a couple of times, and was quite confident that I could put the fly in exactly the right spot when the fish showed. Time passed, and I began to think that I had either been mistaken or the fish had moved on, when quite suddenly the large golden gleam struck my eye again. It showed about four or five yards to my left; I waited some thirty seconds, and then cast out directly in front of me – an easy cast, but one I needed to get exactly right.

Everything worked. The fly plopped exactly where I wanted it, and the leader followed it down. Suddenly that leader jagged two inches across the surface, and I lifted and tightened into a veritable whale.

A quite crazy fight followed, and I'm sure that rainbow fought with double the energy because it felt so cheated and betrayed, so confident it had been of a continued smug life. Never was I happier to have stepped up in line strength, for that fish went just about everywhere. Indeed in those days one of my great failings was a tendency to fish too light. Probably the Silent Man had over-impressed me with the wile and guile of a trout, and I always felt that fishing the lightest leaders possible would give me the best chances of success. But this was not necessarily the case. That rainbow was landed, fortunately, and big it was, but other good fish were lost because I refused in those days to go as heavy as I should have done.

Buzzer Fishing

One of the delights of Brian Clarke's book and a feature of the Silent Man's teaching was appreciation of the buzzer technique. To see a trout eating buzzers – hatching midges – is an absorbing sight. The fish look so lazy and so confident, and they take the insect in such a lip-smacking way, that they seem to cry out to be caught; but things are not always so easy, and when fishing the buzzer the slightest mistake can be deadly.

The first fish that I caught on a buzzer from Edgefield was on a mild, damp afternoon when I was fishing the north bank with the Hall facing me across the water. I remember that a good fish was taking buzzers right in the reflection of the huge, towering chimney stack. I caught that fish on a red buzzer tied to a size 16 because everything I did

When fishing cheek by jowl on small waters, the tiniest considerations put a sensible, thinking angler ahead.

was delicate and absolutely tight. I made sure that every last half inch of my tackle was perfect, and that the cast and retrieve were both just as smooth as silk. That rainbow – a fish of about 1¾lb – took the imitation just as confidently as it was taking the naturals around it, and I was highly delighted with another breakthrough.

However, once again I was somewhat misled, and for a while placed too much faith in the lightest of lines. Two evenings later I was standing on the lake once again, and there was an enormous rise of fish to buzzers as the light began to fade. Gerry was standing with me, watching and obviously suffering as time after time I was losing fish to the artificials. I was fishing superbly – and not landing a single trout. The problem was simply that my leaders were far too light: sometimes these good fish were taking the buzzer, turning their head against the pressure and snapping the line like cotton, almost before I had reacted. That night I lost nine fish without ever a battle really beginning at all, but it wasn't until the next day when I talked to the Silent Man did I realize that I could afford to go heavier in situations like that, and still see plenty of action.

The Lessons Learned

That's how it was in those exciting early days, and though mistakes were made, steady progress was more than outweighing them. As that season wore on I came to know the water and its fish more and more deeply, and my catches rocketed. For example, I knew that fish would often visit feeder streams at certain times of the day or when the temperatures in the main lake reached a certain point. I knew which weedbeds attracted fish and which repelled them at different times of the day, presumably because of food release or chemical imbalance of some sort. I came to know not just the bottom contours but the make-up of the bed itself, where there was sand and gravel and where there was black, dead silt.

All these things built up, and soon I had an almost complete picture of the water in my mind; and I never, ever dreamed of going to Edgefield and failing. Every fish now was planned and its capture thought out to the smallest detail, until I

eventually felt I had reached the level of the Silent Man and never caught a fish by chance or by random casting. A great teacher and an even greater author had taught me well.

EDGEFIELD SCHOOLROOM

In those days as we edged towards the 1980s, I was teaching at a boys' independent establishment in the heart of Norwich. Life had instantly become rather more easily paced after the large city comprehensive in which I had begun my career: perhaps it was because the children were more highly motivated – or perhaps it was just the fact that a far greater percentage of pupils and staff alike were interested in fly fishing!

PS was my new headmaster, an ex-Japanese prisoner-of-war, and one of the best and most religious men I have ever known. PS brought to my Edgefield fishing a whole new dimension: in his presence I slowed down and soothed the fever that I always felt once the tyres bit the track to the lake and I saw the gleam of water in the distance. Before PS I had always been tempted to run to the water, over the meadow, desperate not to miss a vital second on the water: when I went with my headmaster I was altogether calmer.

I remember one particular day with PS in early August just before the 'A' level results were due out – always something of a tense time for both of us. PS, however, sat on a bench on the south bank for two whole hours, never moving, just watching the water, making occasional casts at fish that drifted right into his feet, certainly no more than two or three yards away from him. By lunchtime, I had taken three fish and PS had two. We had drunk half a bottle of claret and eaten our sandwiches, and then he slept for a couple of hours in the idyllic summerhouse that was open for angers' use. I fished the afternoon away, coming close to a couple of good fish but not really making any impression on them. PS awoke half an hour before tea and took his third fish, then a piece of cherry cake and shortly after landed his fourth. He then had to wait half an hour, watching a kingfisher, while I completed my own limit. I don't think we need to underline the lesson learned from that day's fishing with my dear headmaster.

CMR was very different. By profession an English teacher, CMR remembers the period as warmly as I do, and has been kind enough to offer his own recollections of that period:

Norwich Cathedral Close as the spring turns into summer. In the Masters' Common Room conversation turns round many subjects but above all 'Expeditions Day'. What will you do? Stay at home if possible – it's nearly the end of term! Take the boys for beach sports at Cromer! Then with a smile, the new history teacher suggests a House angling competition.

Bliss! He'll organize the whole thing and I haven't fished since I was a boy. I'll come, but I've only got an old Sealey Octofloat split cane rod.

A smile, warmth, encouragement: don't worry, you'll enjoy it. Bring your own rod and reel, I've got all the end tackle you'll need. And so it began: childhood revisited – here was someone to tie the knots and provide the baits and the swims, and above all make you know that you *could* catch a fish.

The competition was magic. A gentle rain was falling, and the boys were almost as excited as I; the swims had been fed up by JB, our new Crabtree. And who cared about the wet? Fish seemed to turn or bubble out of range, or was it simply raindrops?

The Masters' team did not win. Early excitement with a small and horribly slimy eel was briefly transcended by a huge bite on Crabtree's line which was the result of my reeling in to check my bait. Patience, enthusiasm and dedication were Crabtree's traits; I always missed bites, tangled lines and checked the bait far too often. The boys were reeling in bream – lovely, broad, docile fish in their livery of olive-green and gold – and still we had nothing. We talked of this and that, and by the end of the match we'd progressed from being colleagues to friends.

Little did I know how that day would change my life. John drove me home, and over a welcome dram our friendship cemented, even though we were to become Rod Bender and Reel Screamer – he the expert and I the blundering but enthusiastic apprentice.

The day came for our first trip to Gerry Gent's trout lake. In a moment of enthusiasm I had

The boys pose after a successful trip.

Perfect moorland brown trout, four or five to the pound, but often difficult and exciting to catch.

A bay off Loch Lochy; perfect in the summer when large fish will drift in to feed in the rich shallows.

A mixed bag of big browns and char. The average weight of these fish was over 3½lb and all fell to the fly at the end of the season.

An Edgefield brown from about twenty years back. A beautifully formed, deep-chested fish.

Loch Poulary, one of the finest fly lochs in Scotland.

A close-up of a female char
(above).

A very short-lived char
record of 5lb 10oz. Nearly
4lb has been added to that
weight since then, and the
record still climbs.

Tom Boulton shows his prowess on big stillwaters with this fine rainbow.

Reel Screamer Rowe with a fine bag of stillwater rainbows.

A small stillwater in high territory, still home to some good trout.

Joy Hicklin-Bailey hooks into a very large stillwater rainbow and looks suitably pleased with the results.

A sight no one wants to see – but remember a big pike can be a bonus to a trout fishery.

A very fine brown trout of nearly 5lb that fell to the fly.

Woman and dog pose with a beautiful fly-caught trout.

A beautifully marked and shaped fish taken from an English reservoir in the early part of the season.

The scale of trout forms and sub-species is amazing. This trout taken in the early autumn has the white-edged ventral and anal fins that one would associate with a char.

The stillwater trout fisherman's dream (below).

bought a cane fly rod from a dealer who was closing down. I hadn't noticed that it was warped and heavy, but not to worry as John kitted me out with a modern carbon rod, reel and appropriate line. And, yes, he tied on my leader, but gave me a fly and showed me where the stockies swam.

I'm not sure how I managed to cast at all. Somehow the line went out before me even the leader by now was tangled round the point. Next the leader would round the rod; then the fly caught in the top spring; after that everything was tangled in thistles on the back cast. The water was totally thrashed, and the Pheasant Tail had been stripped of almost everything. The deer-stalker took the next assault, but by placing the rod on the ground I was able to extricate the hook from the hat – strange how all those little knots had grown on the leader.

In the meantime, John had gone on hands and knees further round the lake and was crouched beneath the willows, head down, invisible to any fish and casting without any obvious effort above a deep channel which none but he would even have noticed. He watched me and smiled, cast and retrieved, cast again crouched lower and then there was a bend in the rod and a tension on the line and in the air. There had been no back casts, no ripping of leaves, no bending of twigs. The tie point of the line cut through the surface of the lake and John had moved up a bit from the crouch. Right hand lifted and arm flexed as he followed the pull. A fish! A fish! I called out but he did not hear me in his concentration. My line snagged in the weed as I retrieved, totally absorbed in his drama.

Well, I left it like that and hurried to his side, doubtlessly putting down every fish in the lake with the thumping of my heavy boots. His rod was bent right over, but still he kept the tip up, giving and retrieving line, giving again, stiffening his elbow and again giving a length of line, unfrightened by the judder and the shudder coming through the butt, undespairing when the fish burrowed deep in the weed roots, patiently waiting, putting on side strain, walking a few yards to the left or right, easing the tension, turning up the pressure, always confident in his knots, his tackle and his craft. And then, there it was, long and brown and freckled and fresh. And beaten.

Even I could not make a mess handing him the landing net: a beautiful brownie of 3lb. The priest, a snort from the fish and the sweet smell of

water and weed, into a carrier-bag it went, submerged at the water's edge and ready for gutting, stuffing with succulent lemon slices and grilling at the day's end.

Back to my rod. Well, the Pheasant Tail had been thrashed out of all dressing: a naked hook with a bit of a turn and only one tail. The leader was knotted and much shorter than it had been when I started. Patience from Crabtree: a new leader, new fly and some advice about less force, using the action of the rod and cocking the elbow on the back lift. He cast for me and allowed me to make the retrieve. Coils of lime at my feet and total incompetence with the figure-of-eight, that magic of wrist and hand.

No, I didn't catch a fish, not even a poor, small rainbow stocky mistaking the thump of my line for that of a food pellet. But I'd felt the excitement of a catch, and had seen the human heron stalking its prey with stillness and quiet concentration. I had attempted a bloodknot, and knew the aching pain of thrashing the water and gripping the rod too hard. And I can tell you more about John's technique of those days. First, look at the water from afar and, as it were, drink it in. Search the way the breezes play on the surface and see where insects may fall from branches and so where fish may lie in wait. Where do springs or streams feed the stillwater? Second, approach with caution: keep below the horizon and walk gently; do *not* march to the brink and stand upright while you tackle up. Third, never take your eye off the water: something may move, some unexplained ripple will encourage and attract. Fourth, use the lightest tackle you can control in the conditions and which is fair to the fish. Thrashing the water will kill the atmosphere of Gerry's lake anyway. Fifth, always believe the fish are there and can be caught, even if you cannot see them.

As an absolute beginner uncertain of his skill, I gleaned all this from John. When you arrive, try a brown Pheasant Tail until, say, elevenses. Then sit down and have a cup of coffee and a sandwich. If you've seen or felt nothing, change for a weighted green-olive until lunchtime – at which point we would visit the Honeybell.

The light begins to go, shadows lengthen, and plops and ripples show fish on the move. Buzzers, quick! Twisted, skinny, stumpy things. John ties a red one on for me and a green one for himself, and casts to the ripple. I fall short. He misses a

A more formal photograph of this time, pressed against the cathedral wall! The author –
very much younger – is on the top right, whilst the Reel Screamer props up from the left.

take or two, and I probably didn't recognize the suck or pull when it came. The light is going fast and the swallows of dawn are replaced by the flitting, erratic flight of bats. You can hardly see to form the knots and change the fly but still we must get another fish. Tie on a Whisky, a Baby Doll, anything. The latter is best, white with a luminous tail. A fast retrieve, several casts per minute, any tangle on the back lift and I'm done for. And I am! Still, the morning's brownie lies chilled and fresh in the shallows.

As the moon climbs and the twilight fades we walk down with Gerry Gent behind the dam.

Here the clear little stream reasserts itself after its delay in the lake, and greets the water diverted through the stew-tanks. In artificial light we watch a huge eel languishing below the trout, not swimming, or resting, just confused. Gerry does not want to interfere with it, bears it no malice, cannot see any sort of problem or threat. It will find the outpipe, just as it found its way in, and one morning it will be gone. An owl hoots from the copse. We walk up to the car: the headlights break the gloom, the sweet smell of freshwater fish sweeps over us, and the landscape settles down, to awake new-dressed in its mantle of dew.

6 THE JUMBO TROUT OF JURASSIC LAKE

Whilst at Edgefield Hall I made a trip south to a most extraordinary water. It was a July day, very hot and bright, and as I wandered from the car and looked down I thought I had blundered into paradise. Before me lay Jurassic Lake. It was around eight acres (3ha) in extent then, a pit dug some twenty years before, and the water was absolutely crystal clear. And everywhere, criss-crossing the surface continually, I saw big fish – *very* big by my standards at the time. They were pretty well all rainbows, huge cruising spotted submarines averaging 2lb to 3lb but with five and six pounders here and there, and occasionally a much bigger fish again. As a young man brought up on 1lb and 1½lb fish, I really could not believe my eyes.

I stumbled away, quite awestruck, to find the owner and introduce myself, because fishing was quite tightly controlled and it was not simply a case of buying a day ticket. Fortunately he seemed to like the look of me, granted me permission formally, and related a little of the lake's history. He'd had the pit dug two decades before, and in the process they had come across several fascinating remains. The bones of many prehistoric creatures were uncovered, and most excitingly, unknown plant seeds were sifted out that when put in water even began to germinate. The area had become a geologist's treasure trove, and the whole place was accredited with extraordinary powers. Certainly the water clarity and the food richness were remarkable and helped to explain the phenomenal rate in the trout growth. Also the rainbows almost certainly spawned in this pit, one of the very few places they managed to reproduce successfully. During my time there I certainly caught a few fingerling rainbows of the most magical proportions and colour.

It was not only the place and the fish that were so out of the ordinary: so too was the clientèle. What rather surprised me at the time was that the majority of my fellow fishermen were elderly and retired. I suppose in part this was due to the fact that I tended to go mid-week; also the water was expensive, and perhaps day tickets were out of the range of many men struggling with mortgages and families. But the fishermen on Jurassic did not look what I would call out-and-out anglers. This is not meant in any way to be patronizing: what I mean is that their gear was acceptably new and their boots and bags and clothes were overly clean. Most of them had come to fishing late after busy lives in banks, the law or the armed services; once retired, they had begun to look around for something to do and their attention had been attracted to fishing. However, it was not a passion with them, not something to dominate life, but just a hobby. They had no background of childhood tackles and teenage frustrations, and few of them had any real *feel* for tackle, fish and water conditions. Above all, one or two of them showed little tolerance for what they saw as my eccentricity.

Another thing that was noticeable about the clientèle at Jurassic was the fact that nearly all of them worked lures, and nearly all these lures were big Whiskies. There is nothing wrong about this, and there are plenty of fish on the banks all around to prove it, but the strange thing is, it was as if I was not allowed to what I wanted to do, in the manner I wanted to do it – which is why I am telling this tale. . .

I suppose at that time I just looked young to them – it was quite a long time ago! I certainly accepted that I was not catching fish at what they considered the required rate, but as you can

An old shot taken after one of the first trips to Jurassic Lake. The fish, for those days, really were huge. Here is a double-limit weighing something over 30lb.

see her perfectly, and I could see my fly, and it was possible to work it as well as I felt I had ever done before.

In short, I was in paradise, apart from the continuous procession of grey-haired worthies behind me telling me to 'put on a Whisky – that'll do the trick!'

All I could do was smile and nod and turn back to the job in hand; and eventually, three hours after starting, a leaded olive nymph on a size 16 did the trick, and after a quite pulsating fight I landed what in many ways was the very best fish of my life up until that date.

I only landed one other fish that day, and as I prepared to leave, the owner looked at me sadly, presumably thinking I wasn't much of a fisherman. Perhaps he was right, but I did manage to explain to him my technique and approach, and the glorious excitement I had experienced throughout one of the most wonderful days of my early years. One or two of the other fishermen, also packing to leave overheard me and moved closer to listen to what I had to say. We began a general discussion and compared fly boxes, and soon I was being asked all manner of questions; questions I was not really equipped to answer then, but I knew that with diligence my time would come.

JURASSIC'S MONSTER TROUT

It is important to realize that when I was going to Jurassic Lake a big rainbow trout was considered to be about 5lb, and a ten-pounder was a monster. In those days we hadn't really heard of the fish of 20lb and over that now lumber around some of the put-and-take fisheries of England. It is not for me to make any ethical comments here on this type of fishing or on this type of fish; if people want to fish like this it is their business, and if financially viable, then fishery owners will do what they consider best for their clients. What I will say is that the jumbos of Jurassic Lake were not like this: they were fish that had been put into the water when small and had grown naturally, and this meant that they were in peak condition,

guess, I was having the time of my life! I had spotted a quite perfect rainbow of around 4lb (4lb 3oz, to be exact) in one of the really weedy areas of the lake.

She was moving up and down in a very calm, peaceful way, feeding steadily. With all that weed about, the other anglers on the water had clearly not been able to use their lures, and so they had avoided the area – hence the placid fish before me. As far as I could tell it was just me and her, and a battle of wits between us both. First of all I offered corixa, then various nymphs; she was constantly alert and I had several near-offers.

The day wore on and I moved here and there, up and down the bank, constantly following her, putting out short lines every time she seemed to be feeding and nicely in range of a short cast. I could very well aware of natural food, and accordingly difficult to outwit.

I have been to two waters on press days when jumbo trout had just been introduced, and when it was hoped that one or two of them would be caught for the cameras with resulting booming publicity. I have to say that the fish were not as disorientated as I had originally expected they would be, but nonetheless, it was painfully obvious that they were not at home in the water. They did not have well-defined patrol routes as far as I could see, and seemed to be quite easy prey for any good angler who knew what he was doing. This, I stress, was not the case with the Jurassic Lake fish which provided an excellent challenge.

On my second trip, I realized that the Jurassic rainbows were, in fact, rather larger than I had at first estimated. The reason for this is that very clear, deep water often proves deceptive when it comes to estimating the size of fish. You would think – and the old theory goes – that fish would appear larger rather than smaller, but this is not actually the case. In general – and a lot depends on the clarity and depth – fish can be seen anything between 30 and 40 per cent smaller than they actually are; so for example a fish that looks 3lb in the water can very easily be 5lb on the bank. Such was the case at Jurassic.

In fact Jurassic was an excellent example of this type of distortion just because it was so deep and clear. Moreover, the very big fish there tended to spend most of their time in the deepest areas of the lake, where they could be seen only dimly through polaroid glasses when the sun was quite high. Sometimes these big fish did enter the shallows, but not very often at all, and the very best ones never seemed to come much above the ten feet (3m) mark. At first I wasn't sure why this was, because there were quite significant weed growths harbouring a good deal of food on the plateaux here and there. Then I began to realize that the deeper water held some incredibly rich snail beds; two or three of the very big fish that I caught were found to be chock full with snails when opened and cleaned.

The choice facing me was whether to fish a sinking line with a normal length leader, or a floating line with a long leader. I chose the latter, largely because I'd never liked fishing with a sinking line, and because I feel that it doesn't offer nearly as effective a presentation as the floating line/long leader combination. Of course there are times when a sinking like is absolutely essential, but if it can be avoided, then avoid it I will.

In this case the leader I made up was always between 20 and 25ft (6 to 7½m) long; this takes some casting, but I was given the confidence to do this by Brian Clarke's excellent book which describes in detail how to cast just such a long leader. Once the technique has been grasped, then it really is quite simple to do, and there is no real mystique attached.

This time, unlike Edgefield, I did not make the mistake of going too light, and the leader at the point was 5lb breaking strain and never any less. Fly did not matter nearly as much as the ability to get one down to anything between 10 and 15ft (3 or 4m) or so; thus any big snail, shrimp or spider imitation would work quite well providing it was heavily leaded. Sometimes I put a split shot on at the head of the fly to take it down even faster.

I often fished blind, just casting out into the deep areas waiting for a fish, but wherever possible, when the light was bright enough and the surface was unruffled, I would try to choose my fish, casting 3 or 4yd (3½ to 5m) in front of the slow-moving rainbows. Of course it took a certain amount of experimentation before I could guarantee how fast each fly would sink: the idea was to have the fly passing the fish at the right level, a few inches in front of its nose. A fly descending like this the trout often found pretty well impossible to resist, and most of the takes were actually recorded as the fly was on the way down through the water, either to fish seen or fish unseen.

If the fly were not taken on the way down, then it was wise simply to let the floating line drift slowly around the area. Slowly was the key word, and it did not really matter if there was little movement on the fly. Sometimes, possibly to amuse myself rather than for any other reason, I would lift the line and impart a bit of movement to the fly, but that rarely seemed to have any great effect. No, retrieving was hardly necessary, and it

A dramatic jumbo brown!

was as though a trout would simply amble along, see the drifting fly and make up its mind whether to take it or not. But once its mind had been made up, then the take would be as positive and unmissable as anything I have come across in fly fishing: the line would simply draw tight and be pulled under, and all that was necessary was to tighten and the fish would be off.

Those fish did fight very well indeed, and at first I decided I would be well advised to invest in heavier gear. I therefore went out and bought a new rod and reel designed specifically for big rainbow trout on smaller stillwaters; the rod was around 10½ to 11ft long with quite a savage test curve. The reel was a monstrous affair able to take a heavy fly line and well over a hundred yards (90m) of backing.

In fact I found that this heavier tackle did very little at all; because of all the increased pressure, quite frequently the fly would be pulled out of the fish's mouth. In the end I went back to using my normal 9½ft rod with No 6 or No 7 floating line, and simply played the fish that little bit longer. It was important to have a good length of backing on the reel because very often the ini-

tial run or two would take a good deal off, but thereafter it was simply a case of keeping cool and guiding the fish away from any potentially embarrassing snags. In fact, upon reflection and after checking diaries for that two-year period, I cannot recall a single fish that came adrift once it was hooked and I had reverted to using the lighter tackle.

When it comes to the question of really big, 20lb-plus rainbow trout, I personally am torn between finding excitement myself and seeing a very big fish: I find the stocking of small waters with these jumbos something of a commercial gimmick, a thing I decry in angling. However, there is no denying the glamour of a really massive rainbow, especially if it is in peak condition, and there is something very impressive indeed about such a huge fish coming towards the bank in clear water; it is a feat that most anglers can probably manage only once or twice in their careers. This is all I shall say about jumbo fishing, because I don't really think it is in the mainstream of general still-water trout fishing; but if the opportunity does come along, then perhaps the best advice is to make the most of it and enjoy it to the full.

PETER STONE'S WAY WITH JUMBO TROUT

Peter Stone is a legendary Oxfordshire angler who has been involved with the Thames, its tributaries and all the stillwaters that lie in that area for many years, and his tally of bream, barbel, chub and roach is enormous. However, what is marginally less known is his skill with the fly rod, in particular his ability to catch the huge rainbow trout of the southern stillwaters. Few people have Peter's experience of this very specialized sort of fishing. He very kindly contributes an account of his experiences here.

> There are various golden rules when it comes to jumbo fishing. First of all, good quality polaroid glasses are absolutely essential. Jumbo fishing is all about visible fishing, and you have to be able to see into the water as well as you possibly can.
>
> Almost as important is to wear drab clothes and to approach the water as carefully as you possibly can. It amazes me the number of people that you see by the side of these small stillwaters dressed in every way possible to advertise their presence. However, there is no point in risking your chances, so go camouflaged, and be careful.

The flies I use are almost always weighted nymphs of various patterns. In actual fact I carry only a very few patterns, but all of these I have confidence in. Confidence is everything, and is often far more important than the pattern itself.

Having spotted a jumbo – and nearly all my fish are taken by stalking – you have to determine what depth it is lying at. Now in gin-clear water this is not easy at all, and you really have to have accumulated a bit of experience before you can get it absolutely right. You see, if the fish is cruising you have to cast ahead of it so that when the trout reaches the fly both are at the same level. This is critical, because the jumbo is unlikely to come up or go down a long way for a fly.

It is also critical to watch the trout and not the fly. It is probable that at depth your vision of the fly will be shaky anyway, whereas the trout is always going to be obvious. When you see the fish open its mouth, then you strike; you *do not* wait for a pull. The exception to this is when the trout is swimming towards you, and then a strike might well pull the fly out of its mouth – and I speak from bitter experience! You will come to realize that even a jumbo can sip in a fly very gently and expel it again with hardly any signal on the leader, and you will certainly hardly ever feel the take.

Not a jumbo, but it's on its way there!

Always use sensible tackle because these are big fish; they really can work up a head of steam, and stopping them takes some doing. Most times, my leader will be 10lb Double Strength line from Peter Drennan; I find this works exceptionally well. Another thing that I always do is to matt-varnish the rods, because glossy rods undoubtedly scare trout on sunny days.

When I spoke a little while back of weighted nymphs, I really *do* mean weighted here. Virtually all my flies have a weight equivalent of a BB or an AAA. At all times it is absolutely vital that the fly *must* sink quickly so that it gets down before the trout changes its direction. Think about it: if the fly takes a long time to get down to the fish then there is every chance that the trout will have moved right or left or even turned round and started going the other way. When you see a trout's direction it is absolutely imperative to get that fly down to its nose as quickly as you possibly can.

Not everyone has good eyesight. I do, and this helps considerably when it comes to stalking big rainbows. Here is an example: last year I was looking around a small lake when I spotted a 'shadow' in the water. I couldn't make up my mind whether it was a fish, but the longer I looked the less it looked like a shadow. If in doubt, the golden rule is to cast, and this I did: as the fly sank, the shadow moved – and another 'double' paid the price.

There is one last point that I really must emphasize. Despite what many people say, these big trout are *not* easy. All right, some are silly – so are many big pike – but if you adopt that attitude you won't catch any. I think a lot of this misunderstanding arises because so many big fish are put into the water just in time for press days, and they can be quite gullible when they've only just entered the water. Once they've been there a short while, however, you'll find them as difficult as anything. In fact, you should treat them as a coarse angler would treat chub – and there's no scarier fish than that. Yes, a good chub fisher will catch big trout!

And Peter Stone certainly knows about both.

A superb fish goes back.

7 MANAGEMENT OF A TROUT FISHERY

Nearly twenty years ago, David Green started offering trout fishing in East Anglia in a small way, with a lake of no more than half an acre (¼ha) situated in a village near a river. The signs were promising and within a few years he decided to develop a complex of lakes further up the valley. Now, in the mid-nineties, David controls three lakes totalling nearly thirty acres (12ha) of deep, pure, rich water – a trout fisher's heaven. Alongside them wind reaches of the River Bure, a charming little stream which has been left to nature and now boasts a fine stock of wild brown trout that live in deep pools here and there under the alder trees.

David is an expert on the joys and sorrows of running a trout fishery, and what he has to say makes fascinating reading; the following account is in his own words.

THE OWNER'S VIEW

Being a fishery owner isn't easy because you are selling a difficult product. Suppose you are manufacturing something: you price it to make a profit, and sell it, and everybody knows exactly what they're getting. A trout fishery is very different, however. You see, if you've got ten potential customers it would be hard to find two who want exactly the same thing. One will want a great big portmanteau of fish of 12lb plus, and another will want to fish the tiny stream for six-inch brown trout. They are the extremes, but in between there will be all manner of desires and abilities. Some will want to fish a dry fly, others lures; some will want ¾lb fish for the pan, and others 4lb monsters for a family feast. What tends to happen is that on any fishery the owner is constantly apologizing to at least 50 per cent of the punters because they are not getting exactly what they want.

You can try and shuffle things about hoping to provide what more people want, more of the time, but if you do this to any great degree things tend to become even more frantic and you soon begin to lose the satisfied customers without attracting any new ones. It is far better to pick an average angler, see what he wants and try to give him that; in this way most people will get what they want for quite a lot of the time.

Unfair Competition
One major problem that most commercial fishery owners face is unfair competition. Nearly everywhere now, throughout the country, a few miles from any commercially run trout fishery there will be a non-profit-making fishery close by. Round here, for example, we have the Norfolk Fly Fishers, the Norfolk and Suffolk Fly Fishers and all the Salmon and Trout Association waters. These are all admirable, but they are run on a non-profit making basis which obviously means that they can offer their members cheaper trout fishing than I can. It's rather like having a shop trying to make a profit for its owner, and next door a similar shop selling the same items for cost price, not wanting to make any profit whatsoever – there's only going to be one winner in a situation like that. Obviously you then have to think about counteracting the odds in some way or another and bringing down your own overheads so that the cost can be reduced to be as competitive as possible. Most fisheries buy in trout at full size, but the price for these is high; you can cut this cost by buying in tiny fish which come very much cheaper, but then you are entering a whole new minefield.

Rearing Your Own Trout
If the normal farmer has a problem with a cow or a pig he simply goes to the vet, who will either cure it or have it put down. However, if you have two thousand rainbows that just won't feed, it's

no use calling the vet because he won't have a clue what to do. You can take the live fish down to Huntingdon and the laboratories there, and a few weeks later you will get some sort of report. The trouble is the fish will almost certainly be dead by this time; rainbow trout diseases are particularly virulent and generally within two days can prove fatal.

So the fishery owner who wants to rear his own fish has got to build up a knowledge of biology that he probably never had in the first place. He must also keep in an expensive stock of antibiotics so that he can treat suffering trout very quickly indeed. And the only way you can do this is by sprinkling the antibiotics, which are in powder form, onto the trout pellets which are oily; in this way at least some of the antibiotics will stick and get eaten.

Gill infections constitute another major problem. You can use anaesthetic to kill the mites which attack the gills and leave the fish healthy, but you only need the smallest miscalculation, get the whole thing wrong and it's goodbye suffering trout.

So far I've been talking about curable diseases, but there are many viruses for which there is no real cure and which will literally wipe out a fishery. Most of these are kidney diseases such as DKD or PAD, and once a virus such as these gets into the water there is nothing you dan do about it, and the NRA will almost certainly close the site down altogether: no fish will be allowed to enter or leave the fishery, and that's it. There is no cure, and you just have to sit and wait it out.

So there are all sorts of problems with rearing your own fish. Another factor is the space: it's tempting to have the smallest holding pens possible so you are not biting into the fishing area. The problem with this is that if you stock at too high a density the trout will attack each other's tails, which obviously produces undesirable fish. Another problem is that if you crowd rainbows all together they will feel stress, and will be that much more prone to disease. So factory farming rainbows in this way produces unsightly fish, *and* fish that suffer from a high mortality rate.

And you needn't start thinking about insurance, either! The Farmer's Union will not insure against disease anyway, only against theft, and the premiums are sky high. you will be charged at

Rearing your own fish does help, but the problems are extensive.

Everything has to be taken into account if you are opening up a stillwater trout fishery for the public, including facilities for the disabled.

about 25 per cent of the stock value, so you are actually paying the equivalent of another load of trout every four years – something hardly any of us can afford to do.

Predators

Predation is something else to bear in mind when you are trying to work out the profitability of a fishery. The local predators are often of the two-legged sort. Several years ago one particular man cleaned me out of fifty 10lb-plus rainbows that were waiting in a net ready to be trickled into a lake to provide some really super sport. In getting those fish in the net he also released hundreds of immature fish that were never seen again, so it wasn't only the big fish that were lost. Ironically, I was told that he took those fish back and kept them in his bath trying to sell them. He only got

rid of half a dozen or so, and the rest died and had to be buried, so it really cost me a colossal amount of money and made him very little indeed.

We are also plagued by herons here morning, noon and night. The problem with herons is that they will stab fish for the hell of it, and fish that are far too big for them to eat. Nets are really no good at all, and if you try putting them over a holding pen you can guarantee that a heron will find any gap and get in. Also a heron doesn't have to wade to catch its food. Many is the time I've seen a heron land in one of my nets out over deep water, simply letting its legs sink and putting its wings out to hold it up; then it will just start looking around and stabbing fish as they swim within range.

More recently we've been worrying about the cormorant issue, too. This really is serious, and Brian Clarke wrote about it recently in *The Times*. As he said, there has been an extraordinary increase in the cormorant population on our inland waters, and there are probably about twenty thousand birds nowadays in England and Wales – a number that is increasing at somewhere between 6 and 16 per cent per year.

Clarke is right when he says that cormorants eat a pound to two pounds (⅓ to 1kg) of fish a day. Now that means quite a sizeable loss to me if there are a dozen or so cormorants on my waters. Overall, the damage to the country is staggering and he is right to say that something like twelve hundred tonnes of freshwater fish a year are being destroyed by cormorants. That is a colossal amount of fish, and is hurting wild stocks of coarse fish and the pockets of fishery owners, large and small.

Clarke also makes the very relevant point that it is not just the fish killed and eaten that are causing us all headaches: a great many trout are just wounded by the cormorants because they are too big to be eaten, and these fish continue to swim around, slowly dying. Clarke gives some most revealing figures. For example in Grafham water in Cambridgeshire, of 718 trout caught in fly fishing competitions, 300 – or 41 per cent – showed actual cormorant damage. If you think how serious these figures are on a huge water such as Grafham, just consider what a threat cormorants are on a small water like mine. And, believe me, waters like mine are the vast majority. For every big reservoir there will be at least forty or fifty small fisheries struggling to make a living, and the cormorant is one of the major thorns in our side.

Predators are a curse. Just what killed this fish, for example? Possibly a stab on the shoulder by a heron, but what finished the fish off?

All walkways like this have to be made as safe as possible with wire netting, otherwise a costly insurance suit could follow.

Very soon we will have to be allowed to cull them to some extent if we're going to stay in business. The trouble is, cormorants are such greedy birds and will gorge themselves until they can't fly. They are also clever, and work in gangs; one will act as a lookout whilst the others feed, and they will take it in turns like this. Sometimes a cormorant will simply fly round and round the lake while its pals feed and it keeps a real bird's-eye lookout.

Tickets, Rules and Costs

The whole method of charging on commercial fisheries is a minefield, and one that drives every fishery owner crackers. I think it was Alex Barendt who began the crazy scheme of charging ex number of pounds for anglers to catch and take away ex number of fish. This seemed all right at first, but it gave rise to many problems, and from the angler's point of view there was only one good thing about it. An expert could concentrate on catching, say, four big fish and if he caught them, he was really fishing for nothing because the value of these fish often more than paid for his ticket. But this was at the expense of the novice or the not-so-expert, who were in actual fact paying for his fish because ticket prices had to reflect the expert's catch.

One problem is, in these days of recession especially, that fishermen often travel a long way which is expensive, and come with a limited budget. Let us say that they pay £15 for a four fish bag. They start all eager at eight o'clock in the morning, and within two hours they have their four fish. What do they do for the rest of the day? Do they pay an extra £15 to catch another four fish, or do they go home? It's a major problem to them and to us. Some of them will pack up, and some of them will pay for another ticket, but many can't afford it and don't want the extra fish anyway.

The problem is that not all trout anglers are honest by any means. Suppose no one has seen you catch the four fish: you can easily drop one behind a gorse bush for the rats to eat and nobody is a whit the wiser. That gives you another fish to catch, and you can repeat the process throughout the day.

Another trick is to see the beginner walk past and to ask him if he has had any luck. Often the answer will be no, and it's a simple matter to give him four fish so that he checks them out for you, and you can

carry on fishing without having to buy another ticket.

This is yet another scenario that often happens: let's say a small trout is caught and killed at 8.30am; then at nine o'clock another little one is caught, but slipped back. By six or seven o'clock in the evening the expert angler has probably kept one small fish and three big ones and slipped back twenty or so little ones. This means that the fishery owner is out on the price of his ticket and has probably lost at least half of the small fish that were released.

The fishery owner is constantly trying to work out how many fish of what size the average angler catches. If everybody played by the rules, calculations like this would be quite possible, but because there are so many cheats about – and you've got to call them that – prediction is invariably out of the question, and every fishery owner has to operate to some extent in the dark.

All this is tied up with catch and release, and many anglers ask why catch and release can't be operated on stillwaters as much as it is on many rivers. My general answer is that it isn't, largely because of the way trout are treated these days. They are shown scant respect, believe me; there is almost a complete absence of the old rules and behaviour that I used to see twenty years ago. In those days it was usual for a lad to be taught by his father or grandfather, and a lot of good values would be passed on. Nowadays this doesn't happen, and people come to fishing without any real guidance, just picking up what they read in magazines or papers. They regard fish in a very cold, hard-headed light, simply as things to be caught. I'm always coming across people who don't even bother to kill their fish, but just let them flap around on the gravel by their side so they can get back to fishing that little bit quicker. And you try talking to these people about careful handling of a trout without lifting it from the water, nipping it or maltreating it in any way!

So catch and release just isn't going to work in most stillwaters with the sort of customers that you get these days. So many of them are ignorant, and will handle fish roughly or squeeze them, fish that are already exhausted from fighting. The other important consideration is that stillwaters do not have the amounts of oxygen in them that rivers do: if you put back a tired rainbow trout that has been treated badly, then four or five times out of ten this fish will simply sink to the bottom, not move, take in less and less oxygen and finally keel over and die. At least in a river you can put a fish back facing the current, so that a lot of oxygen will pass through its gills, and it will probably swim off quite strongly after only a few seconds.

So to sum up, although catch and release sounds a good idea, it is not actually practical at all on most stillwaters where people don't know what they're doing. And if you try to *make* a ticket holder treat his fish well, then you will very soon be accused of stroppiness and unpleasantness and not making people welcome, and they will clear off and go somewhere else and wreak havoc there.

For all these reasons I have introduced the sporting ticket on my waters. Thus people pay solely for the privilege of fishing; they can catch as many fish as they like, and then they leave them here with me at the lodge and I sell them on. I'm lucky that most hotels and restaurants will take them off my hands, providing the price is about right, and I estimate this stops ninety per cent of the cheating – and you can always offer the fish back to the angler at a discounted price if he wants them. The only possible drawback to this system is that the fishery owner has to make that extra effort of selling the dead fish; but in my view this is a small problem compared with all the other ticket types that I've studied and even implemented in my time.

Common Errors

For twenty years now I have been walking round trout lakes day in, day out, watching thousands of anglers perform, some very good, most about average and some horrendous! Casting is frequently a barrier to catching fish. Some anglers just love casting, and take great pride in showing how much line they can put out; they'll spend 80 per cent of their time with the fly in the air, and will catch hardly anything at all as a result. At the opposite end of the scale is the man who thinks trout are stupid and will thrash the water with his line with every forward false cast – sometimes I've seen foam around his feet, but there hasn't been a trout within a hundred yards (90m) of him.

The crucial difference between the true expert and the normal average angler will be his ability to sense a take. I'm absolutely convinced about this.

Most trout, and especially the less-than-hungry ones, will simply follow a fly out of curiosity. I expect 95 per cent of flies that are actually taken are not done so out of hunger at all, but simply because the fish wants to see what they're like. Now in most cases, the trout will merely nip the fly for a very short period of time before rejecting it, realizing the thing is not at all edible. Most anglers don't have even an inkling that their fly has been investigated in this sort of way; the true expert, however, has some sort of sixth sense and for no apparent reason will tighten and be into a fish.

I have no doubt in saying that the best fisherman here is a man called Stephen who comes from one of the coastal towns. He will average twelve fish when he's not even trying, and always on nymphs and buzzers. I've watched him fish, and the only thing that puts him above everybody else is this uncanny ability to know when a fly has been engulfed.

Let me tell you this story from my salmon fishing days and you'll see what I mean. When I was about seven my uncle ran the Exe Valley Fisheries. This was just before the war, and I used to go down and stay with his son, my cousin, who has since spent all his life in fishing in one way or another. Anyway, this cousin was quite a bit older than me, and a very good salmon fisherman and he fished the Exe a lot. One of his favourite spots was the Black Pool, the junction between the Exe and the Barle. This is a very deep pool indeed, but when the light is right and you lie on the rock above it you can actually see the salmon in the water.

One day my cousins took me down to the Black Pool just to watch fishermen from the Caernarfon Arms tackle it. We lay there watching all morning seeing anglers come and go, all unsuccessful. What they didn't know was that on at least twenty occasions salmon actually came up from the depths, came to the fly, drifted downstream with the fly in their mouths and then ejected it without any indication whatsoever; as far as the anglers on the bank were concerned, they hadn't had a single touch at all. So they all went home, and then my cousin took out his rod and began to fish. Every time I saw a salmon come up and sip in the fly I would simply put my thumb up and he would strike. In just a couple of hours he had six fish this way.

The method actually caught on, and people realized what I was doing and they would pay me

A view of the Exe Valley fishery.

very good pocket money indeed to sit on the rock watching their fly, and telling them when to strike. I suppose a lot of small boys make a bit of money on the side, but I suspect this is one of the most unusual ways yet.

Winter Fly Fishing

I do believe in allowing people to fish for rainbow trout on stillwaters in the winter if they want to, because I don't think they are doing anything or anybody any harm at all. Rainbows here feed all the year round, and certainly through the coldest winter weather, and the fishing is probably better in the winter than it is through most of the summer.

I have no qualms about this at all because the rainbows are 'artificial' anyway. In the wild, a trout should be five times as long as it is deep, whereas here, because of artificial feeding, they are probably only three times as long; you can see that they are man-made fish, and so they should not be subject to the good rules we put down for wild ones.

Rainbows are much more susceptible to high temperature ranges than low ones. In summer, once the temperature gets to 60 or 70°C, the fish will have no appetite at all; if they do feed then it will be very early in the morning, and they will

Maintaining a trout fishery to beautiful standards takes time, effort and expertise.

spend the rest of the day moving as little as possible, just enough to allow some water at least to go through their gills and keep them alive.

Cold temperatures, however, don't bother them and I have seen great feeding activity even when the water temperature has been approaching zero. In fact I have considerable problems here as there are warm springs which enter the lakes and keep the ice off in a few places; the rainbows leap through these holes and then find themselves skidding along the ice, unable to get back into the lake. I have to get into a boat then, and hack my way to them and return them before the seagulls can get them!

So a winter rainbow is much more likely to feed than a summer one, partly because the water suits it better and partly because there is very little natural food in competition. Also the water is colder and there is more oxygen in it, and so the fish fight and look better anyway. So as far as I can see, if an angler wants to brave the cold, then let him. Believe me, fly fishing on a cold, crystal-clear frosty morning is quite an experience, and something I would recommend to anybody.

PIKE AND THEIR PLACE

The pike is the traditional villain of any trout fishery and it is easy to see why: pike are undeniably responsible for the death and maiming of a certain percentage of fish. Historically, it seems that putting a pike in a privileged trout water was a way of getting even: the famous Dowdeswell pike was allegedly dumped into the water by an irate angler in the 1880s because he was not allowed to fish on a private water that was reserved for the trout-fishing town councillors of nearby Cheltenham. The pike grew enormous on trout in this reservoir, weighing something in the region of 60lb in its prime. So quite obviously trout are a popular item on a pike's menu!

All of us have known the disappointment of feeling a take, only to reel in a 2lb jack; or even worse, seeing a decent trout on the end of the line being savaged by a pike on its way to the net. Nothing is more infuriating. If you are a member of a trout fishing club yourself there is the added frustration of knowing that a percentage (even if often exaggerated) of all the stock fish that you have paid for, goes down the great maw of this most ill-regarded species.

It is therefore hardly surprising that pike in trout waters have suffered from years of persecution. In Scotland this is still the case, and in recent years I have witnessed fisheries' boards laying nets over the mouths of pike spawning bays through April and May and disposing of the carcasses as best they could. Dead pike and even perch are a common sight along the banks of all UK fisheries, tossed there by disgruntled anglers to rot. In Ireland things are possibly even more serious, and a recent Irish angler of my acquaintance who had just landed a 26lb pike on Lough Mask admitted that he had to kill it or he would have feared for his life; certainly he would not have been welcome in the bars for a good many weeks to come!

All this hostility is understandable, and at times even justified; if a new trout fishery is being created it makes sense to try and ensure that pike do not get into the water, and occasionally this can be successful. However, we just have to accept that in many, if not most waters in the United Kingdom, pike are a fact of life; and even more to the point, once pike are in a water it is almost impossible to eradicate them, and indeed any attempt to do so can increase the problem.

It is now scientifically proven that the killing or removal of *all* pike can be counter-productive because big pike, fish of 12 to 15lb and above, tend to eat a great many small pike of between a few ounces and 3 or 4lb; indeed small pike are almost certainly the *preferred* prey of large female fish. In a fishery it is the small pike that do most of the damage, snapping at trout, ripping them, but unable to kill them cleanly. If the large pike are removed, then you remove the main predator that will control the small ones, the nett result being that these proliferate. This scenario has happened repeatedly in water after water, and thankfully, many fishery owners are beginning to see the sense of allowing big pike to stay alive.

If culls are to take place on any trout water, it therefore makes sense to remove all fish up to about 12lb, but to *return* pike that are over that

A massive Lyng pike held by Dan Leary. These pike that live off the rainbows grow extraordinarily heavy and fast.

weight. There are rarely many of these particularly big fish, and remember they will act as guardians for you, policing the small jack pike which do so much harm.

The Norfolk Fly Fishers' lake at Lyng was a very good example. In most years the club stocked about 7,000 trout, and in an average year something between 6,000 and 6,500 trout would be caught by the members; this meant that about 500 trout would 'go missing', perhaps victim to winter kills or disease. Perhaps many of these remained alive and were uncaught. All in all, it seems that pike were hardly the problem they are often suggested to be, in this water at least; and this is particularly relevant because, Lyng was a nationally famous pike water. Finally, it is interesting to note that the committee's policy at Lyng concerning pike changed dramatically over the years: at first *all* pike were killed or removed and small pike became a nuisance; then in later seasons the big fish were spared, and very soon the problem of too many small pike dropped dramatically.

There is no doubt that pike do thrive in trout fisheries, and that this can benefit the fishery owner in a positive way. Why they do so well is not entirely clear, especially considering the fact that big pike prefer to feed on small pike. However, recently stocked rainbows are notoriously foolish and tend to swim in shoals, and it is virtually impossible to deny that a few of these don't get quite easily snaffled up. This extra food item almost certainly makes a great difference to the condition and size of the pike – trout-water pike are invariably quite extraordinary fish, being exceptionally heavy for their length. To many anglers these big, broad, beautiful pike are highly desirable fish, and this fact can be turned to the fishery manager's advantage: from October to March, during the close season for most stillwater trout, coarse anglers are willing to pay a great deal for the privilege of fishing trout waters for these big fish. Indeed, some of the famous trout waters which open to pike anglers have waiting lists yards long, and applicants sometimes have to apply for tickets a year in advance. So, trout fishery owners, wake up to the fact that a valuable resource may well be swimming in your waters during those winter months.

There is another possible bonus: pike anglers are willing to pay for livebaits, so why not grow on a certain number of small trout to sell at a great profit to these visitors on your water? There should be little risk of annoying the regular trout anglers, as very few trout will fall to live – or deadbaits, or even to large plugs and spinners; occasionally a big rainbow or brown will be caught in this way, but the number is amazingly small, I assure you. And, anyway, if these fish are around in a water before Christmas it is quite likely that they will be dead before April.

There have been very successful experiments at opening trout fisheries to the pike man. I have mentioned Lyng, but Llandegfedd, Ardleigh and Bough Beech are a few more of the many waters where pike anglers come in to swell the coffers throughout the otherwise gloomy winter months. In nearly every one of these cases the pike anglers have only proved to be a bonus, and certainly the bailiffs at Llandegfedd have spoken very highly of the bankside behaviour of coarse fishermen. Also, the fact that these big pike get caught in the winter months and make news in the angling press provides a great deal of welcome publicity for trout waters – and all of it is free. We live on a very small, very crowded island and it seems only right that all tastes, wherever possible, should be catered for, especially if there is no clash of interests. This, surely, in most cases is the situation with pike in stillwater trout fisheries. They are a fact of life that we must learn to live with, and which actually can be turned to a positive advantage.

Never forget that a big trout is a mean predator itself.

8 THE LAKE AT LYNG

For many years the Norfolk Fly Fishers' Club was considered a role model for similar organizations around the country, and wherever I went, people were very eager to hear about the water and how it was run. The club had been founded in the 1960s by a group of dedicated and experienced members, and by the 1970s the water had sprung ahead of others like it. When I first tried to get into the club there was a waiting list of many years, such was the popularity of the place, in fact I had to wait a good while to take my turn. Sadly the water is no longer controlled by the club and has reverted to coarse fishing.

In retrospect, I think I approached my stillwater trout fishing apprenticeship in the right way insofar as I made my new start on the smaller waters before going on to Lyng. The water at Lyng posed far greater problems in many ways even though it was well stocked with excellent fish.

LYNG CONSIDERED

The lake at Lyng is a forbidding place and certainly I found it so when I first began there. It is around twenty-five acres (82ha) in extent, with all manner of bays and features but still a great deal of water which cannot be covered with the fly. It is an open pit, as indeed most of these types of water are, since it is too soon for trees to have colonized the banks. Quite an innocuous breeze, therefore, can raise a ripple, whilst a wind will produce a noticeable chop. Visibility at Lyng was frequently affected by algal growths which could be appalling in the summer, especially as the fertility of the pit increased. This was partly to do with the proliferation of wildfowl on the water, and also probably the gradual seepage from heavily farmed fields over the years. These algal growths, combined with the muddying effect of wave action, made it very hard to see individual fish, especially as they generally kept some little way from the bank. Of course, rises were widespread on calm evenings from late spring through to the end of summer, but in those early days the fact of the matter was that I found myself confronted with a very large tract of seemingly hostile water, and my major problem, coming as I did from small stillwaters, was simply where to find my fish.

Robbie walks to his fishing lake; he was one of the guiding geniuses behind Lyng's success.

I was a member of Lyng Club for seven years and fished it a lot, especially in the early seasons. I learned much, partly through my own experiences but largely through the help and advice given so freely and spontaneously by the membership. This friendly attitude was a real feature of the Norfolk Fly Fishers' Club, and one that fishery owners would do well to encourage everywhere.

Locating the Fish at Lyng

By the end of my stay in the club I had worked out a strategy for finding fish that worked well on most occasions. Finding fish on bigger waters is one of the most daunting aspects when setting out. At Lyng this was exacerbated by the club's stocking policy, which was excellent: they did not simply put out bucket-loads of fish here and there in large congregations, but took the fish out in a boat and made a dribbled release all over the lake so they were really well spread out. This meant there were not the great shoals of rainbows that are so often found lurking in the bay nearest to the stockpen, just waiting to be decimated.

The Influence of Wind and Currents

One of the most significant considerations on a water the size of Lyng is the wind. Richard Walker always advised to fish as often as possible with the wind into the face, and there is a great deal to be said for this advice. Let me elaborate: the pike at Lyng pit – which were enormous – would generally be found in the north-east corner of the lake, because most of the winds blew from the southeast and that was where waves and water tended to pile up. The pike were presumably there because it was where most of the prey fish were, which naturally included the trout. Thus it was to the north-east region of the lake that I would often make my initial progress; although there were, obviously many other considerations.

For example, on occasion it was very useful to have a good brisk wind behind you, because this would give an only adequate caster like myself the ability to reach features that were known to be particularly productive. One instance springs to mind when a group of brown trout had taken up residence on the lip of a plateau some thirty-

Happy is he who can teach his wife to fish! Audrey Robbins retrieves a nymph.

five yards (31m) from the south bank. They could be seen humping at last light and occasionally flashing during the day as they took an insect, but there was no way I could put out a line that far without the help of the wind. Once the wind came from the south at force 3 or 4, however, then I was able to explore the area, and invariably picked up a fish or two.

Wind also does unexpected things, even on waters 'as small' as twenty acres. I was alerted to this by that excellent coarse fishing writer, Tony Miles; it was Tony's experience that on many of the larger waters where he hunted roach, location was the key, as it is for trout fishing. And what he found central to solving this problem was the power and direction of the underwater currents that the wind set up over the course of a few days. However, there was no indication of these currents on the surface, and he could only pinpoint them by walking round the water casting out an empty swimfeeder and seeing what happened to it on its descent. If the feeder was pulled strongly by underwater currents, then he would settle down to fish there with some hope of finding roach.

This consideration I took with me when I set out to find fish at Lyng, and indeed the advice did work. On hard days when no fish were showing, I would try casting a sinking line; if I saw it drift quite noticeably on its way down I then knew I had found an underwater current, and if I fished this area, very frequently it would be particularly productive – and the only possible reason could be that push of underwater current.

Knowledge of the Bottom Contours

Knowledge of bottom contours is vital. Early in my membership at Lyng I was lucky enough to be given an echo-sounder to tinker with, and I immediately asked for permission to launch a boat and set off charting the water. I found that the bottom of the lake at Lyng exhibited extra-ordinary variations, with sheer drop-offs, a maze of bars and deep channels and many very shallow extensive plateaux. New pits, I believe, are dug on slightly more organized lines – although it would be wrong to expect a profile like a farm pond, even so.

The contours are only important insofar as they affect the trout's life and behaviour in ways that interest the fisherman. It is, therefore, useful to know where the bars lead, because the trout definitely follow them for a considerable extent. Clearly when there is a midge-hatch the trout will go to the surface zones, but when all other things are equal, say on a cold day in April, they will not always travel randomly but choose to follow the bars as routes around the water. This was certainly my distinct impression when I fished at Lyng.

However, let us look at some of the obvious features and see how they relate to trout catching. Plateaux can be excellently productive areas. Because they tend to be shallow, and because silt often gathers on them, they tend to grow the more luxuriant weedbeds in the water; this promotes insect life and also attracts spawning

Beautiful stock fish always count for a lot. Jack Fitt was fishery manager at Lyng, and reared the trout from fingerlings to release with stupendous results.

coarse fish. The great bream shoal at Lyng numbered some huge fish amongst its members, and would always use a shallow plateau for spawning – and eggs were always mopped up eagerly by the waiting trout. As the fry hatched, too, they tended to stick in the plateaux weedbeds and so the trout continued to hang around that spot. The message, therefore, is quite obvious: if you find a plateau, then you ignore it to your own disadvantage.

As I mentioned, Lyng had enormous drop-offs where the depth would plummet from just 2 or 3ft (¾ to 1m) down to 18 to 20ft, (5½ to 6m) within a yard or so. These areas were well worth knowing about because they undoubtedly attracted fish, browns especially, during hot and sultry summers; down 20ft (6m) or so it was comparatively cool and the light was dimmer. I don't suppose there was a massive difference (I never took water temperatures in those days), but it was a help, and enough to focus a lot of fish in those deep areas which could just be reached by a quite fast sinking line.

Lyng was fortunate in having several margins with shallow sloping edges, and there were also numerous bays dotting all the banks. There was no doubt that the fish, browns especially, came in close to feed in the dusk, through the night and into the early morning before moving off into deeper water. Any angler who stayed late or appeared early would profit by fishing these areas, as long as he made an extremely careful approach to the water's edge. Big fish especially used to haunt these places, and at first light it wasn't unusual to see them rolling, very impressively, in water as shallow as a foot.

So when faced with a water like this it is useful to know the depth variations because they dictate weed and food, light and temperature, and all the things vital to a trout's comfort and survival. They are one of the keys to puzzling out exactly where a trout will be living.

Other Features
Naturally there are other considerations: at Lyng there were numerous islands, and trout did work these, hugging the margins closely where the trees overhung. Even more important at Lyng were the semi-sunken islands; these were the outcrops of bars that still sported the odd bush or dwarf tree but were being eroded all the time by wind and wave action.Often these small islands would disappear during the course of a season, but even so there was a good deal of them left under the surface and trout were attracted to them as if by a magnet. Presumably there was plenty of food on the roots and branches that were dying away, and it was this which drew the fish in.

Eventually a pipe was inserted from the nearby river into the lake in order to bring in fresh water and help combat the algal problems. The river water, from the Wensum, generally ran at a slightly lower temperature than the stagnant lake water, and in summer periods especially it was not unusual to find a good number of fish stacked up where the cold oxygenated water met the warmer lake. Also the fish almost certainly liked the extra push of the current, besides any titbits of food that were swept in from the river. However, in my experience this immediate area was, surprisingly, not quite as productive as everybody once thought it would be: certainly trout were there in greater numbers than elsewhere, but it was still not the goldmine we all expected.

Much the same could be said of the bay where trout for future stocking were kept. This was netted off from the main lake and the fish in there were fed two or three times a day. Obviously not all the pellets were eaten instantly by the captive trout – or the ducks that congregated there – and many drifted or floated into the open pit; one might reasonably have expected a good number of released fish to have gathered, therefore, in the immediate area. True, a good few did, but again, not the hordes that theory would have predicted. This is interesting because in various other waters I have fished, the trout pens do seem to be real magnets.

The clubhouse seemed to be nearly as big a draw, just possibly because of all the lunch fragments thrown in by overfed anglers.

Other little features had their attraction from time to time: for example on the south bank there were areas of thick marginal reed that frequently attracted some quite big fish, especially at dusk when they seemed to come in and browse on the stems for snails in particular. Equally attractive at times was the bridge from the south bank onto the main island, and for some reason a number of good trout would gather underneath it, seeming to like the shade it offered.

You might say it is impossible to describe the average pit and I can appreciate the criticism. The important thing is for the angler to be aware of everything around him, to consider all the options that are open to him and the fish. It is vital to make some attempt at rationalization, and not to fish in a fog of blind hope alone. Of course, there is still a lot left unexplained about a water such as Lyng, and just finding the fish does not guarantee success. However, if fish can be contacted on a fairly constant basis then the chances are infinitely better than if you are fishing areas of barren water where the odd trout simply travels through once in a while.

LYNG STRATEGIES

The Fly Fishers' Club at Lyng was a super organization in every way. Not only were the stock fish excellent, but you were also allowed to catch them when you liked. The rules stated that eight fish each week could be taken, but if you wanted you could fish all seven days for them. Above that there was a hundred fish limit for the season, and this allowed me to visit the water two or three times a week hoping for a fish or two each time. As a result, I got to know the water at every time of the season and in all its moods. I never got to my hundred. This was largely because there was

no pressure on me actually to catch fish: all that race for the four fish limit was removed. Season after season I was quite happy with a tally of sixty fish or so, as long as they were caught in ways that interested me. So what Lyng offered was a great feeling of freedom, and the opportunity to experiment with every sort of fly fishing on offer.

With over a hundred members, all sorts of techniques and skills were on show, and everybody wanted to master the art of dry fly fishing, nymphing or the delicate presentation of imitators: the lure-men were well represented, and probably the foremost of them was my dear friend Billy. Even back then Bill was past retirement, but he was just as keen on fishing – whether for pike or trout – as any man a third of his age. He had been a teacher, and I guess a highly respected and loved one, but fishing now was his major preoccupation and the Lyng water offered him very serious trouting

Pawsons Senior and Junior: stillwater fishers who have set the world alight. Both champions, both generous with their advice.

indeed. As far as I am aware Bill always stripped back lures. He had a strange technique that I've never actually witnessed anywhere else: the rod handle would be shoved tightly under his right armpit and that left him both hands free with which to retrieve. The speed of that retrieve was frightening – or at least it frightened me! It didn't seem to put the trout off, however: year after year Billy caught his hundred trout before I was much out of single figures.

In general Billy would not cast too far, but used a slow sinking line and quite large lures. I still think it was the speed of the retrieve that worked so incredibly well for him – far better than anybody else who fished lures on the water at that time. There were a few who half mocked him – though only half because Bill was such a

marvellous friend and genuine human being, and in the end, you hardly saw any derision at all of his results. And finally, Bill enjoyed his fishing, and that is how he wanted to catch his trout; and those are the important considerations. It was just the same when it came to pike fishing the water in winter: whilst the rest of us would live-bait, Bill was quite happy with a deadbait – even though for one memorable five-year period he fished every hour available without recording a single run! Perhaps he should have gone back to lure stripping.

Jim Knights, Writer
One of the most important influences on me in the early days was Jim Knights, a well-known angler and writer in East Anglia. I'd only been a member

A typical Lyng rainbow held by Roger Miller. Member Reg Sandys looks on. Reg is a long-time boat partner of Bill Giles.

of the club a matter of weeks when he lent me his rod, as he said it was already made up and he just wanted to relax in the hut for an hour or so. It puzzled me at first why he wanted me to take his gear rather than my own, but I soon saw the reason. I think he had appreciated that my own tackle was clumsy by comparison, and this was a gentle and tactful way of letting me see the difference.

Certainly Jim's rod and line cast far more sweetly than my own. This was partly the fact that the quality was better, but also I realized he looked after his lines more conscientiously than I did mine. Whereas I had let mine be damaged by sand and allowed them to crack, this was not the case with Jim's and I realized the difference in casting ability immediately. Being able to cast sweetly meant of course that the line lay far more tidily on the water than ever mine could do. I also appreciated Jim's leader, which was long and beautifully tapered, with none of the clumsy knots that I was content with and had used for a good number of seasons. And there were his flies: as I remember he had a small weighted nymph on the point, and a corixa or similar on the dropper: imitative flies on tackle that could present them perfectly.

With Jim's tackle I managed to hook and to lose two trout in the short period of time before he re-emerged from the hut and gave me a cheery wave. I walked back round the bay and handed him what was left of his gear with a rueful smile. 'Sorry, Jim,' I said. 'I seem to have lost quite a bit of your gear. I'll make it up, of course.' Jim simply roared with laughter, shook his head and hoped that I'd had a pleasurable half hour. It had been more than pleasurable!

Tom Boulton, Match Angler

Then there were the mid-way men, such as Tom Boulton, the well known Norwich tackle dealer and match angler. For much of Tom's fishing life he was on the bankside to catch fish: niceties were all very well, but results counted, and this was the very effective mentality that Tom brought to Lyng. For example, one hard cold day in April when I was struggling badly, Tom wandered across and pressed into my hand a big, black, evil-looking Dog Nobbler.

I was stunned. This was the first time that I had actually seen such a creation, and although I had heard and read of them, I had never quite

Wise fishery management allows the bank cover to grow high.

appreciated the scale of their devilment. Jim showed how to cast them without fear of decapitation, and how to work them in a sink-and-draw fashion close to the bottom. The day was revolutionized: takes materialized out of nowhere, and what takes they were – savage and wholehearted, and soon I had four fish on the bank beside me. Equally, on the long, balmy evenings of summer, Tom was just as adept at creeping round the south bank where the scum of the day had collected, picking out individual rising fish on the tiniest of buzzers with the most delicate of points.

Tom was a busy man with an expanding business and parents to look after, as well as a rising career in the match world: he couldn't afford the luxury of spending two, three or even more evenings each week wandering around Lyng sampling this and that: he liked rather to go home with a bag full of fish, and it was rare that he went away without his limit. I appreciated this, and learned from Tom that different seasons and different days demand a constant variety of methods if fish are to be caught regularly.

Jack Fitt, the Purist

Finally there was the purist, Jack Fitt. Jack was a long-time hero of mine. Back in the 1950s roach meant everything to me, the great 2lb roach from the River Wensum that were making news all over the angling world. Back then, Jack Fitt had once landed twenty-six 2lb plus roach in one afternoon session. I had heard of that and at the time had been quite stunned, a motivating reason for joining the Lyng Club was so that I could meet Jack and talk to him, when I could, about his roaching exploits.

Jack was (and at the time of writing still is) the fishery manager for the Norfolk Club, and his stocking regimes were quite exemplary. Although most fish bought in were very small, they were then reared through a whole system of closed streams and pools before being released into the lake. The result was that the fish were supremely fit, healthy and acclimatized, with not a stubbed tail in sight. The problem for Jack was that he began to love these fish like his own, almost as children; after all, he fed them two or three times

a day even through the winter, and cared for them through diseases, and I truly believe he felt for them every time the priest descended.

As a result of this Jack didn't care to catch too many trout; or if he did, it had to be on his own terms. He would only ever fish for his trout on the dry fly, and this of course restricted him considerably. Still, when conditions were favourable, principally after a warm day from May onwards, it was not unusual to see Jack walking slowly and carefully round the water, in part to chat to members and in part to look for a steadily rising trout. I don't know how many trout Jack caught each season, though I expect it wasn't very many – but that is not the point: his satisfaction was in knowing that every single one had been caught to his own personal rules and in the way he wanted to take them.

Special Fish Remembered

There were many fish caught during those happy times that meant a great deal to me. The vast majority just came along and impaled themselves on my hook without my ever really knowing why or how; the line would just magically tighten and I would be playing a cartwheeling silver fish with my heart pounding. There were, however, very many times when I realized I'd pushed my own personal boundaries that little bit further forwards and actually caught a fish as a result of skill and rational thought. Let me give a few examples.

The Elusive Browns

Early one June, a group of good brown trout in the 2lb bracket had taken up station in the slightly deeper water just out from the mouth of a bay. Almost certainly these fish were used to coming into the bay during the hours of darkness to feed on the very rich pickings there, and in the daytime melted out to where the water was deeper and offered more security. In short, these trout had a very slow, steady, almost circular route which took them out into the lake, round a while and then back to the lip of the bay where it was just possible with my casting abilities to present a fly to them. The problem was that if I made long cast when they appeared, the force of the line

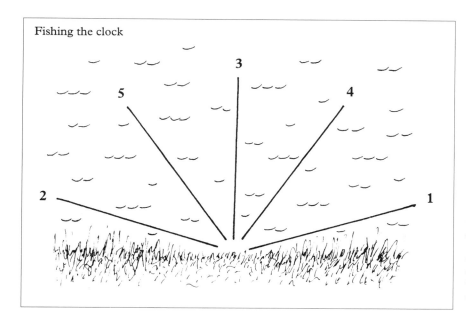

Fishing the clock

Fig. 27 On many reservoirs, especially cold upland where food is not plentiful, trout often keep on the move, and it pays to be mobile and to keep working the bank until you come across them. It is also a good idea to fan the casts out in roughly the order that is shown here; in this way you will cover the whole area of water in front of you, and by varying the position that you lay the line down, you are less likely to scare fish and generally upset their territory. This is only a subjective pattern, and you can vary it to suit your own whim and the weather conditions on the day

hitting the water would invariably be enough to disturb them and drive them back out again. I therefore had to think of some way round this.

I discovered the answer was to wait for quite still days when I could make a long cast and leave the line for some minutes sure in the knowledge it would not drift out of the killing zone. The leader was a long one – again to try and disguise the presence of my tackle – and quite heavily greased. The fly would almost always be a quite heavily weighted black and peacock spider which I knew would sink down four or five feet (1½m) to the bottom.

As soon as I was aware that the group of trout were approaching – normally because fry would sheer out of the way, or a fish would roll, or there would be a dash of yellow – I would begin to lift the black and peacock steadily and quickly, although I would wait until I was quite sure the fish were right on the area. The trick did not work every time; about once in three or four attempts was the average, but it was surprising how many times the eye of a passing brown would be caught and the fish would turn and the fly would be engulfed. Over the course of a week I took four of these fish, browns that everyone else had pretty well discounted. It was quite slow fishing, but the

adrenalin really flowed when those fish appeared and you began to draw on the line!

After a while the technique stopped working, and I assumed the fish had moved on altogether. However, I was intent on browns at that period and I soon found either the same group of fish or a different shoal altogether a little further down the lake. These fish were caught very occasionally at quite great depth by anglers using lures and sinking lines; this was not the way I wanted to catch them myself, however. The weather was quite hot – it was July – and daytime temperatures frequently climbed well into the eighties, the lake shimmering under the bright sun.

Dawn Fishing

It was during this period that I began to rise around three-thirty and make the half-hour drive to the water, arriving as the sun was just on the horizon. The lake then was a different place, and especially this area where the browns were known to reside. Now, at this early hour, they were not in deep water at all but feeding quite vigorously in the shallows. Once again I used a large black and peacock spider twitched gently through the area where there was most activity. Once again takes were positive and assured, and one or two of the biggest browns I ever caught on Lyng water came my way those beautiful dawn mornings. That, I used to reflect, was the true way to catch those fish. All right, they did come out occasionally deep down on lures and sinking lines, but all that sort of pressure made them twitchy and neurotic, and even more so because some were foul-hooked as they lay doggo in the daytime heat and brightness. Perhaps I was being arrogant, but I felt I was somehow tapping into the browns' natural lifestyle, and so each fish I landed gave me that extra stab of thrill and enjoyment.

Fishing Difficult Situations

The water at Lyng was superbly cared for. Way out in the bay from the clubhouse where the extensive shallows stretched, a small fishing platform had been constructed. Members were allowed to sign for this platform for an hour at a time, and to use one of the boats to row themselves out, tie up and fish in perfect isolation and seclusion. The shallows stretched for long distances all round and it was an area I adored, especially in the mid-evening when the light was off the water and the fish were beginning to creep in from the surrounding deeper water to feed in these weed-rich shallows

There were, however certain problems associated with fishing from this platform, notably the weed itself. If a heavy fly were fished too deep and twitched back it was a matter of constantly pulling it free and clearing strands of vegetation. The method I learned to use there took advantage of the wind, which almost always caught the lake that far out from the bank: I made sure that I had my highest floating line, and greased the leader enthusiastically so that it floated without any problem. My fly would be a nymph – it didn't matter which type particularly, as long as it was tied to something like a No 16 and without too much lead – fished between two and three inches (5 to 7cm) from the surface, just enough to

Lyng browns frequently over-wintered and grew to extraordinary size.

skate over the sub-surface weed and not foul up at all.

I would cast across the wind, and then simply let the line drift, working the flies rather as a float man on a river trots his maggots. All I would have to do would be to mend the line every now and again so'that it did not 'belly' too much, and perhaps give the fly a little lift or a twitch. Takes were ridiculously confident, and the leader and even the fly-line would simply shear off against the surface current, and often there was no need to strike, you just had to lift and start playing the fish.

I used something very similar to this technique down at the in-flow pipe when the fish in the area were on buzzers. I found that they would be very reluctant indeed to accept a buzzer cast straight into them, even when they were feeding hard. So the method I adopted was simple: I would cast into the flow of water coming into the pit, then just let my line float with the running water until it reached the taking area. That way the trout were not disturbed by my casting one whit, and it seemed to make all the difference.What I truly believe is that those trout very quickly became aware – at least within a day or two – of flies and fly lines and flaying rods and casting fishermen, and they knew that such things meant trouble. My very low-key technique avoided many of the actions that alerted them, and so was remarkably successful.

The Giant Rainbow

I managed to take very few of the leviathans that occasionally Lyng was stocked with. I think that probably if I'd used lures, things would have changed, but not many big fish came to my small nymphs, buzzers and dry flies. In fact I can only remember one real monster, and that came in May after a group of big fish had been found in the south-west corner of the lake, where anglers had given them a real bashing; over two or three days I should think fifteen to twenty rainbows all in excess of 4½lb (very big fish in those days) had been taken from one small area. There were still fish present, but they had become very wary and extremely difficult to hook. Occasionally one would snap at a fly, but more out of irritation than anything else, and it would invariably be lost almost instantly. Quite

obviously the shoal of big rainbows had broken up, and although not all the fish had left, they had become neurotic and fidgety.

Very close to this area the major bridge from the south bank led over to the big island, and I began to spend a certain amount of time watching this stretch, looking straight down into the quite clear water. The shadow of the bridge itself helped fish-spotting activities, and I began to realize that every now and again – say, every half an hour or so – two or three big rainbows would swim hurriedly past. I emphasize hurriedly, because these fish were obviously quite stressed and not moving at all in the way of placid fish intent on the odd meal. When they came, they were travelling about three or four feet (1 to 1½m) from the surface, and I decided to put on a large heavily weighted damsel fly nymph and wait and watch. After some twenty-five minutes, a group once again came into vision (there seemed to be three or four distinct knots of fish). I cast – it was really just lowering the fly down from the bridge – about three yards (2¾m) ahead of them, into what I guessed was going to be their course. The fly sank quickly to a depth of about five or six feet (1½ to 2m) and when the fish closed, I began to twitch it violently up and down. The take was instant and I found myself being played by a big fish indeed; it began to take me round the back of the island, and I had to scamper off the bridge onto the south bank, passing my rod from hand to hand around a couple of poles. The fish was just everywhere, diving into weed, leaping clear of the surface, pulling line off until almost all the backing was gone and the rim of the spool was exposed. I was quite literally shaking; never had I wanted to catch a trout quite so much – or at least not for a quarter of a century!

Gradually, yard by yard, I retrieved line as the fish began to tire. At that moment, another grand character came into my fishing life: Vic Bellars, veteran of a thousand campaigns, who appeared with a long-handled landing net to help me at the final stage, and with evident pleasure at my whoops of joy, swung up onto the bank a fine 6lb rainbow.

Lyng days: never, ever will I forget them.

9 RESERVOIR FISHING

Tom Boulton is better known as a major tackle dealer and one of the country's leading match coarse fishermen. However, for many years he has been a very keen and extraordinarily skilful fly fisherman, especially on the big reservoirs of the east and the Midlands.

Tom's fishing is typically down-to-earth: like the matchman he is, there are no frills attached to his style, and he considers fishing as a job of catching. This is particularly the case when it comes to reservoir fishing, which involves the expenses of travelling and buying tickets; besides the loss of time, his first concern is to make sure that his days on the reservoir count to their fullest effect. The account which follows is in Tom's own words.

RESERVOIR FISHING: A REALIST'S VIEW

There is no doubt about it that if the average angler wants to catch a trout or two from these great big reservoirs then the early part of the season is probably the very best time to try. It might be pretty rough and windy and cold, but the trout are in there in some numbers and most of them are pretty stupid and quite catchable.

The main problem in my view is always going to be location, especially in these early months when there isn't a fish showing anywhere. Remember that the fish are never scattered about like currants in a bun, but tend to be shoaled up quite tightly in little groups. Okay, you will be told with absolute certainty that there are plenty of over-wintered fish available in the reservoir for you to go at, even if you don't find one of the shoals of freshly stocked fish, but don't put too much faith in those. Over-wintered fish tend to be much more discriminating, and especially with the cormorant menace that

seems to be growing each year, I'm not quite sure how many fish are getting through. No, it's the stockies that you've got to concentrate on, and that means finding one of the shoals. A lot of that will be down to local knowledge: amongst the locals, the news gets around like wildfire that there's a big group of fish here and there, and you tend to find that anybody in the know goes straight to the spot and starts banging out fish.

If you don't have this information, then you've just got to keep your eyes open and see where the action's going on and try and get as close as you can, or keep on the move. Obviously you wouldn't move out of a hot area where you are getting lots of takes, but if there's no action, keep going and keep going! You can spoon fish at this time of year and the food that they have in them is absolutely minimal, perhaps just a few blood-worm if they are lucky. It is for this reason that the rainbows tend to shoal densely, because it takes them quite a while to find a feeding area so that they can at least get something. So in my view that's going to be the biggest problem for the average angler – simply finding the fish to catch.

Tackle

At this time of year, certainly for the first month or six weeks, the fish tend to be crazy for lures. Remember that it's basically stockies that we're talking about, and there isn't much natural food anyway so the time for nymphs and dry flies and all the rest comes later on when the weather improves.

For lure fishing, I always like a sinking line, either weight-forward or with the shooting head. Long casting is important, and I don't care what anyone else says about it. You get a lot of talk about how the trout come in close, and that's true, but they don't do that after fifty-odd people have been in front of you splashing and wading about, catching fish and disturbing everything. The trout aren't going to be by your feet then, they'll have cleared

The bleak expanse of a Midland reservoir.

off a fair way, I can tell you. It's all right if you're one of the celebs who are invited to the press days – you'll be able to catch fish wearing trainers a yard from the bank; but everything changes the next day when the hordes are let loose.

Of course, you can put a long cast out with a size 6 floating line, but you need to be able to cast long distances hour after hour, and so you need the kit that will let you do it as easily as possible. Probably, therefore, I myself would prefer the shooting head even to the weight-forward as it's cheap and it involves you in minimal casting effort. Of course, a shooting head is bad for presentation and I'd never say otherwise. But once the fly has sunk fifteen feet and it's absolutely sheeting down with rain and blowing a gale, presentation isn't really the problem that it is in the summer when you're inching a buzzer about, is it?

So in general terms, I'm looking at a rod between 9 and 10ft, something capable of casting lines between 7 and 9 or shooting heads between 8 and 10.

With the leader, I'm looking to fish one as long as I can handle without getting into a muddle and

Wading can give a slight advantage, but frequently the fish close in are disturbed.

tangles all the time. Ideally I'd like one around nine or ten feet long, but if that's not really possible six feet will do, and I'll just splodge it out into the waves. I'd rather get a short leader thirty yards out than a long one five yards out, if you see what I mean.

Leader strength is something to bear in mind, and in the early season I fish heavy without any qualms at all. After all, these are stocked fish and they haven't seen much before, and possibly the next thing they'll see is a frying pan! I don't bother with anything like double-strength lines, and I like a good stretchy mono because the fish will hit like dynamite. The minimum leader size I will use is 6lb but I sometimes go up to 8lb.

Think about it: you are using a quick sinking line and you're pulling the lure in fast and the trout will hit it *really* hard – after all you're probably pulling the lure through a group of twenty or thirty or even more fish, and perhaps a dozen trout see it and make for it. The one that actually gets it is the fastest off the mark and will probably make off with it in the direction opposite to the one you're pulling in! You can get the mes-

sage . . . I've had 8lb line break like cotton on fish that have been pretty ordinary, and I've caught them later with my fly leader in their mouth.

Stock fish in a shoal are quite different to the type of trout you'll meet up with later in the season when everything's settled down and there's natural food about; then I begin to wonder about their intentions towards a lure anyway. Of course, there's nothing new in this, and there's been long debate as to whether a rainbow trout wants to eat a lure or if it's just attacking out of devilment. Whatever the reason, they really hit it with a wallop, and you're left in no doubt that you've just had a take – certainly when your line snaps!

Lure Choice

When it comes to lures, I try to be as basic as possible and not confuse the issue – something I see a great many people doing these days. Customers will come flocking into the shop and they'll read one magazine or another publicizing yet a different lure pattern, and that's all they can think about. What they don't seem to realize is that

It always pays to keep an eye open on big waters like this. Just a little surface movement might give all the clues you need.

Reservoirs at the start of the season and well into the summer can be very busy places.

people make a living out of writing about these weird and wonderful things, then tying them up and selling them. There's really no need, and you can stick to the basic lures and catch just as many fish, in my view. All you need are a few lures that are basically black, white and orange: as far as I am concerned those are the main colours, and they do me nearly all my lure fishing

Obviously the sensible angler will always weigh up water conditions: for example, the coarse fisherman wouldn't use a single caster in a roaring flood on the Severn, would he? So it's no good fishing a sparse little black lure if the water is twenty feet deep, the sky is overcast, rain and wind have coloured everything up and there is a real storm breaking. Then you'd be much better off with something bigger and brighter with a bit of light and flutter like a Maribou. If, on the other hand, you've seen fish moving perhaps in shallow water where it's quite clear and there's not too much wind, you should choose something a bit smaller

and a bit sparser that looks a little bit outrageous.

So, when it comes to choosing lures, just stick to the basics, use your head a little bit and try to keep a clear view of all the hype and rubbish that goes around on the subject.

I love taking a walk round Ardleigh reservoir in the early part of the season; there's one bank where you can walk along to see people catching fish, and they'll have two or three on the bank beside them: you'll ask them what they're catching on, and they'll all say black lures. Then you'll go round the point to the next piece of water and the same thing is happening – people playing fish with fish around them. Ask them what they're taking on, and here the answer is white lures! Now, you're not telling me the rainbow trout have changed their preference just because you've turned the corner: no, it's just what people are throwing at them – because one guy is successful with a white lure, everybody else follows suit and catches fish. Remember, they're just stockies, and don't be intimidated by them.

Boat Fishing

If you can, it always pays to get a boat, even in the early part of the season when fish are catchable from the bank. The great thing about a boat is that you are mobile and you can see very well what's going on, and where people are particularly catching fish.

The great thing about a boat in my view is that you can moor it about fifty to seventy yards from the bank with the wind behind you, and then cast easily into the water that bank fishers can't reach. You're casting virtually always to the bank, and it will almost certainly be empty bank because there are very few anglers who really like to fish into the teeth of a gale. You are all right though, because you've anchored your boat up and are simply using it as a fishing platform. Obviously you wouldn't anchor up opposite bank anglers because that's really bad manners, but you'll find lots of good water that you can fish this way. Do be careful though: if the wind has travelled over half a mile of water it will be picking up some speed, and you must be very careful of big gusts in April if you don't want to go over the side. Also keep a wary eye open that your boat isn't drifting because you could find yourself in trouble on rocks. Never, ever go out without adequate safety clothing – don't even think of it.

Later on you can use a boat on the reservoirs loch-style, and then they are lovely to drift in, moving around, searching for the fish; but in April it's three-overcoat weather, and you use the boat as a platform and very little else. I will often take a boat, especially if I can share it because the way I look at fishing is very realistic. If you've taken a day off work and driven a hundred miles these are two major expenses to start with. You've probably had the day booked for a week or two, so you can't afford to pick and choose and then the day might turn out to be desperately bad. Therefore you need every option you can, and to be able to make the best use of your time on the water. Some days you're there and you know all the locals are still in bed and wouldn't dream of venturing out; but you made the decision to go and you've just got to do the best with it.

I suppose that's why I like the early season fishing on the reservoirs because I don't live close, and I know that the locals don't have any massive advantage over me. After all, this is the time when the trout will feed pretty well all day, and if you keep your eyes open you'll certainly find a few groups of fish willing to have a bash. Also, most people sling out a big lure, whip it back and get a few takes during the course of the day. It's exciting, but not too demanding stuff providing you can stick the weather.

Later Season Fishing

Things change a lot during the later season, and this is when the locals begin to dominate. They will know all the good spots, where fish are holed up in numbers, probably by now feeding on natural food. This means that the fish probably feed hard during the night and switch off about seven o'clock, and the locals know this. So they will be out on the water about four, fish until seven and then be at work just about at the moment you arrive. Even if you know the good spots, you'll probably be lucky if you even get a pull all day long. You'll be leaving about seven o'clock in the evening, a bit fed up and disgruntled, stopping for a drink before making the long drive home – just as the locals are leaving the pub and going down for the last two hours before dusk. And you can bet they'll be catching fish again!

If you can only fish during the day and you've travelled some way, then in my view a boat is a must. In the high summer, if there are to be any feeding fish at all, then they will probably be in the breeze, and nine times out of ten you will need a boat to get there and fish it properly. Indeed, there's not a lot to beat drifting on a nice ripple in decent weather, fishing loch-style with light lines and small flies and pulling out a fine fish or two. That really is great, but of course, you can't rely on the breeze, and sometimes you can come badly unstuck if you make the long journey to the reservoir in the summer.

So to be realistic you've got to think things out a little bit. This is how I like to organize the day: I'll leave work about four o'clock in the afternoon when most of the customers have been through anyway. The drive will take perhaps two or three hours, depending on which reservoir I am visiting and so I'll be starting to fish around about seven, when the first of the locals is appearing! I'll fish right through until about ten o'clock, and the chances are that I'll have had some really nice fishing, catching on the buzzers, imitations and even dry flies perhaps.

Boat fishing obviously gives an advantage when it comes to covering territory.

Then I'll be in the pub about ten o'clock, hopefully for a meal and a couple of pints, and then at eleven-thirty I'll drive somewhere down a lane and have a snooze in the back of the car. If you organize the back seat comfortably this shouldn't be too big a problem. You'll only have about three or four hours anyway, because in June or July the day starts getting light by half three, and by four o'clock you'll be back on the reservoir, with all the locals.

Like them, you'll be fishing for trout that are feeding really hard, often in the shallows, and it's all exciting stuff. I'll pack up, as they do, round about seven o'clock, which means I'll be back in the shop at about ten o'clock in the morning in time for a coffee and a chat with the first really good customers. Okay, by the end of the day I'll be feeling it a bit and I'll be looking forward to an early night, but at least I'll have had six hours or so of really good, successful fishing – and that's what it's all about. On some reservoirs they operate half-day tickets so the plan won't really have cost me any more money, either, which has also got to be taken into account.

So, broadly, that's how I approach reservoir fishing, and it's in much the same way as I tackle a match. I simply weigh up all my best chances, and the best and cheapest ways of bagging up and doing at least as well as the locals. The good local is the yardstick: if, as an outsider, you come near to his success, then you can really pat yourself on the back.

RESERVOIRS AND A ROAMING STRATEGY

Staying in Wales one year I was fortunate enough to meet a well-known local fly fisherman named Owen. First of all Owen introduced me to some tiny hill lochs, usually involving a long walk over moorland, and producing a number of 8 to 10oz fish. After a couple of days of this, he suggested a trip to a mighty reservoir, situated high up above Porthamedog.

We left the hotel after breakfast, as apparently an early start was not too vital for Owen's style of fishing; besides the reservoir is a bleak, comparatively barren place and does not respond in the same way as low-lying waters. Even though it was July when we made our visit, the wind was still quite keen at that altitude and I don't think we saw a fish rise throughout the day. However, Owen soon taught me how to get to grips with the fish there.

His method revolved round lure fishing, using black and white lures of different sizes and textures. They were the only colours he would bother with, starting out with black and only turning to white if success was unforthcoming. The lures were fairly large, at least 1½in (3¾cm) tied on quite sizeable hooks and used with a sinking line, quite a slow sinker on this particular occasion as it was summer, but a faster sinker, Owen assured me, in the colder months. The sinking line simply allowed him to fish the fly at a greater depth variation without having to bother too much with different lengths of leader. As the wind tends to be fairly constant on a lake like Trawsfynydd, long leaders are not necessarily a good idea.

The main priority, as Owen impressed on me that day, was to keep on the move. Because the lake is comparatively barren, the fish rarely concentrate on feeding areas for any great length of time but tend to drift around picking up what they can find and then moving off again. For the angler to remain static, therefore, is a bad idea, and this assumption did seem to be borne out by the fact that there were some bait fishers who did not move all day and only managed the odd fish or two, although you would have expected the worm to be very attractive indeed. Owen's method was apparently much more successful.

It depended largely on the casting arc. His first cast would be to the right, about four or five yards (3½ to 4½m) from the bank. His second cast could then be to the left, about the same distance from the bank once more. His third cast would then be directly out in front of him, straight into the reservoir itself. His fourth cast would then be at two o'clock, that is between the first and the third cast. The idea behind this was to test the water in front of him as quickly as possible, for any fish that might be present. Also, it made sense to lay the cast down like this so that the next

Reservoirs are big places and it pays to be mobile, either by boat or on foot.

cast would be made in a different direction and would cover a different area, well away from the impact of the first cast and any bad effects it might have had.

Owen was meticulous about counting the fly down before making any retrieve. The first five casts would see the fly retrieve quite close to the surface, after he had counted just a single second. Then a second cast to each point would be made after three or four seconds, and the third cast to each of the five points would be made after around six seconds. This would mean that in all, Owen made fifteen casts at each point along the bank, at three different levels. In colder months he would count down to as much as ten or fifteen seconds. This technique meant that a good deal of water was being covered, and if he had any intimation that fish were present – either a fish properly hooked or just a nipped fly – then he would remain put and investigate the area more closely, often changing the fly over if he felt there was something wrong with the original pattern and that a new one might improve things.

Once a particular area had been fished out, and assuming there had been no indication of any fish present whatsoever then Owen would move between 35 and 40yd (32 and 36m) along the bank and start the same procedure all over again. He was helped in this by the fact that we were fishing mid-week, and also Trawsfynydd is a huge water so bank space is rarely at a premium.

On average, we met with fish every about eighth or ninth move – probably every 300yd (275m). I have no doubt that this nomadic way of fishing paid off, and our results that day were far in excess of any of the other anglers, particularly those who remained close to an access point and hardly moved from their original spot.

Owen introduced me to the buoyant fly that day, in this case a black lure made buoyant with a piece of cork on the shank, near the head. He fished this on a surprisingly short leader and a rod set up with a fast sinking line. He merely cast out, let the line sink quite deep and twitched the fly back slowly. This gave the fly a sink-and-draw movement that the fish, once located, would find irresistible, and certainly takes were very dramatic indeed.

There are two more points worth noting about the day: first of all, Owen stripped the flies fast. The reason for this was that because the water was particularly clear, the fish could see the flies easily and he felt they were more likely to attack something they did not have enough time to examine properly. The other point about the fast retrieve was that the casts took less time to work out and therefore more ground could be tested... the key to success. The second matter of interest was that in one particular cove I noticed a lot of very small fish were present. I could not quite tell what they were, but I'm certainly aware that some quite big rainbow trout were persistently cruising just out from the margin, a few yards away from them.

Now, as bait fishing was allowed at that particular time I determined on an experiment: one of the small hill lochs that Owen took me to was absolutely crammed with tiny trout of a couple of inches in length. The next day I climbed to the moor and caught half a dozen, which I then took down to the reservoir that afternoon. I found the bay, and sure enough the big rainbows were in the same position, just out from the small fish. I expected immediate results when I cast out one of the small dead trout and fished it back sink-and-draw: amazingly I didn't hook a single fish, and there wasn't even a take. Through the polaroids, I watched the rainbows show complete disinterest as the small browns moved through them.

I hasten to add I conducted this more as an experiment than a means whereby to empty the water, and it made me wonder even more about the success of Owen's lures. If those trout weren't interested in real small fish, then why were they so easily caught on the big fast-strip lures?

STALKING THE 'WILD' RAINBOWS

Terry Beale is one of those excellent fly fishermen who work effectively and quietly in the background, running clubs and organizing trips and speakers, generally for scant recognition or praise. Terry and I were discussing the fascination of wild trout in wild places, trout that had to be approached with the most delicate of tackle and techniques. We share a mutual affection for Devon, especially the River Barle, and talk began to move towards the grilse runs there. Then Terry proposed that equally exciting fishing could be had on Wimbleball reservoir, close to Dulverton. I also knew Wimbleball to be a real treasure, and what Terry had to say about it was fascinating:

> I obtain a great deal of pleasure in fishing for trout of all kinds. However, limits of recently stocked rainbows from lowland reservoirs do not give me much satisfaction these days unless they are caught by casting small dry flies or emerging nymphs to rising fish.

For me, the best fishing nowadays is found in pursuing wild fish from remote wild places – so you will understand my frequent visits to western Ireland, for example. However, for the last few years I have developed an approach to reservoir fishing which started on the upland reservoirs in England and Wales and has proved to be effective on other reservoirs as well, including concrete bowls such as Farmoor.

Wimbleball reservoir in the Brendon Hills in Somerset is fed by streams in which some of the native brown trout still breed. These brownies can be seen rising in the margins and around weedbeds even when the rest of the water is quiet. One day I deliberately set out to catch some, scaling down to size 4 line, a 2lb point and sizes 16, 18 and 20 dry flies. As Wimbleball can really be classed as an

Two 'wild' rainbows. What do you think?

What a fish to catch!

upland water, I found that black was the most effective colour, although in June, a white Caenis imitation also worked very well indeed.

Over many trips I caught several browns, but I was surprised to begin catching superbly conditioned rainbows as well. These were silvery fish, much slimmer than usual and with tails like shovels, and believe me, they fought like daemons – I had fish of just a pound running out to the backing at unstoppable speed on several occasions. It sounds ridiculous, but it happened.

These rainbows ranged in size from about 12oz to just over the 2lb mark, and I have several theories as to their origin. First, they could be fish that are bred naturally in the lake or in the side streams. This is highly unlikely in my view although I do know that rainbows have bred successfully in a few British waters. The second theory is that these are fry that have escaped from the fish farms higher up the valley, probably from Wimbleball itself. This is a possibility, and it would explain how much they have developed into such magnificent fish, if

they cut out the stew-pond stage almost altogether and fed naturally in the large water from infancy.

The third possibility that occurs to me is that these rainbows could be fish which have been pricked or perhaps have been returned; and because of this trauma they have reverted to feeding entirely on natural foods, and know to flee from the usual fishing tactics employed by the majority of anglers. This I feel is quite probable, and certainly we all know of rainbow trout that after one scare have lived apparently charmed lives for months to come.

My own feeling is that these superb fish are the result of a combination of the second and third hypothesis. Moreover I have found that this stalking technique has worked well at far more waters – for example at Blagden, Draycote and Rutland – and in all of them I have found a percentage of what I term my wild rainbows. So, these magnificent fish are obviously not a phenomenon confined to Wimbleball alone, and I dare say that small percentages of stocks at most reservoirs are of a similar ilk.

10 THE CHALLENGE OF LOCH FISHING

When I first travelled north to Scotland and west to Ireland I was terrified by the size of the waters that confronted me. They were way beyond my previous experience and I felt massively intimidated... at first. Nevertheless, I soon burned to build up the same sort of understanding as I had achieved on my small local estate lake. Obviously such a thing would not be nearly as easy because of the sheer scale of water and the difficulty of seeing fish. However, I was very fortunate that my life changed course around the late eighties and I was able to spend four years concentrating on four or five big Scottish lochs. In fact, between 1982 and 1988 I might spend fifteen or sixteen weeks each year on these massive waters. I am not saying that these extended visits made me an expert, but at least I began to pick up pointers.

UNDERSTANDING LOCHS

When a great deal of time is spent in one place or following a particular interest, you don't learn everything at once but little by little; like a huge biological jigsaw puzzle, the pieces begin to fit together and various clues lead you to at least a partial understanding of what is going on... or might be going on! The first thing I learnt is that these big waters – commonly five miles (8km) long or more and at least half a mile (¾km) wide – are not what we can strictly term stillwaters, or hardly ever anyway. When I was experimenting with char fishing I came to realize that there was nearly always a severe undertow even when the surface was calm and had been so for several days. When jigging for char you lower the flies down to the depths above a large lead weight; over and over I found the weight would not be

heavy enough to go straight down to where I wanted it because the underwater currents kept lifting it and moving it away from the vertical. At times, and certainly when the wind had been quite high, I found that it needed a weight of up to 2oz (57g) to take the flies down without trouble to the level I wanted to fish. I repeated this type of experiment in many different ways, and the results seemed to be the same: beneath the top few feet of the surface layer a great deal of movement is taking place, which cannot be predicted from the surface. Sometimes, for example, the underwater currents are working against the wind, and sometimes they are flowing with it. In short, it is almost impossible to know what is going on beneath the surface.

My own feeling is that this has a tremendous influence on the movement of trout throughout a large loch. The well known coarse fisherman Tony Miles found exactly the same sort of thing when fishing reservoirs for roach; his approach would be to get to the water and move around, casting here and there with an empty swimfeeder until he found the most movement. He would then concentrate in this place, knowing that the roach shoals would be looking for some sort of push of water. He postulated that they looked for these underwater currents because food was brought in to them in a convenient fashion. On that score I would not like to comment, but certainly it does seem that in essence he was right, and that roach in reservoirs like the underwater currents, of which there are many – that is the important point.

So, considering that the big lochs of Scotland are riddled with these underwater currents, do trout actually follow them? I was to learn more about this as the result of a strange offer of employment I received in September 1991. A

An old print of trout fishing on Loch Lomond, a water well known from Victorian times.

large estate owner wanted some research done on one of his lochs both on the salmon populations and the head of ferox trout. He contacted a scientific body who employed me to travel north, live on the water and simply fish my days away – though certain small scientific tasks were, of course, expected of me in return. The most exciting of these was the fitting of a radio transmitter into the stomach cavity of any ferox trout I caught. These were tiny, pellet-shaped things which were inserted very easily and appeared to do the fish no damage at all.

I was lucky enough to catch a number of ferox trout, and performed the operation successfully on each occasion. It was then a comparatively simple matter to locate these fish with a radio on the surface. I had expected that the trout would take up positions in certain lucrative areas – say around headlands, or close to char shoals. This was not the case at all, however, and what I did find was that the ferox kept almost constantly on the move,

never really still as far as I could tell, and covering miles of the loch day in, day out. As far as I am concerned, therefore, ferox trout generally have no particularly consistent holding areas on a loch. Of course there are a few exceptions to this, which will be mentioned, but as a general rule you might as well travel here and there around the water, fishing as you go, just hoping that your path coincides with that of a large fish.

Now, does this actually contribute to any real understanding of loch trout? Perhaps the very big fish operate on quite a different basis from the smaller ones. After all, many writers and experts talk about the best places to look for loch trout, and it would be foolish for me to contradict all that has been said and experienced before. We have to agree that there are certain areas which attract the normal loch trout at certain times of the year or times of day. However, the ferox trout experience could well apply to smaller fish, at least some of the time. I can think of numerous occasions when I have been trolling on big Scottish lochs and have actually followed a rising brown trout for half a mile or maybe more down the loch. There is no evidence whatsoever that this fish has any particular territory, and all the evidence available seems to suggest that it is simply on the move, through the surface layers, taking insects wherever it finds them. That, of course, is when the trout is near the surface and can actually be seen. The big question is whether the same behaviour takes place when the trout is down deeper, feeding on the sub-surface food forms. My own belief is that in many cases trout operate in the same way, on the move, feeding opportunistically as they follow the underwater currents.

This does rather fly in the face of traditional loch lore; however, there are many times and situations where specific areas of the loch are particularly attractive to the trout. At these times it actively searches them for its own benefit. For example, the weedy shallows are often attractive to trout both large and small in the height of the summer when there is a great deal of insect life contained there. Bays and shallow margins are, therefore, always worth searching out from May right through to the end of the season.

It is also true that certain bottom contours nearly always have at least a few trout around them – or that seems to be the case, going by many weeks of using a fish-finder on these large lochs. Such areas are generally situated around rocky outcrops where the water plunges to a considerable depth; trout will be found fitting in close to the bank, making use of any rock ledge. Equally, it is fair to say that trout do haunt promontories, those areas where the bottom runs out quite a way into the loch, providing a broad, shallow band in otherwise deep water. Trout are nearly always found along the sides of these underwater structures.

Many lochs have considerable inlets or arms, too, winding sometimes half a mile into the

Waters like these need a great deal of reading.

Three successful anglers come in at the end of a long day.

surrounding hillside, gradually shallowing and petering out. Very many trout seem to like the junction of the arm with the main loch, possibly because the currents are less strong here, and it gives them some stillwater in which to group and even rest. That, of course, is mere hypothesis, although the fact remains that these areas are usually quite fertile in fish.

Other evidently attractive spots include stream mouths later on in the season when the trout are thinking about spawning. The smaller, ordinary brown trout invariably use different streams from the bigger ferox, which is how the genetic integrity of the ferox is maintained. In all probability, any ordinary trout moving into a ferox territory as autumn approaches would be either attacked or even eaten. Man-made structures provide a focal point, too, notably fish cages on the loch where a certain amount of food almost always filters

through the nets, uneaten by the parr or smolts within. Char shoals certainly gather round these places, picking off what filters down to them, and trout also make use of this unnatural bonus.

What, then, is the net result of all this? Well, I would certainly recommend boats to head for areas where anglers have done well in the past, because it is highly probable that a bottom feature or a weedbed will always hold a greater-than-average share of trout. If the angler has done well in the area before, then he is likely to fish with greater optimism and therefore do well. However, I still feel that gradual and fairly haphazard drifting will also pay dividends – providing of course, the angler is fishing the right method effectively. At the end of the day, you see, I believe that large percentages of these great loch trout simply drift, using the currents, feeding as they go, and you are quite likely to run into fish almost anywhere on the water.

FISHING FOR WILD BROWN TROUT IN SCOTLAND

This section has been very kindly provided by Malcolm Goddard, an angler who is quite expert on the larger Scottish lochs which he has come to know extremely well:

> For the angler who ventures in search of something just that little bit different, often there appear to be no short cuts to success. Fishing in alien surroundings often presents a multitude of uncertainties that the visitor has no means other than persistent trial and error with which to achieve a successful technique. Thus the holiday angler may spend so many hours constructing a winning formula that by the time fruition has brought a radiant glow to his cheeks, the fishing time available to him has been hugely depleted.

In Scotland this occurrence manifests itself painfully clearly. The scenic splendour and solitude with which this country is blessed attracts anglers from all over the rest of Britain to fish its waters for wild brown trout. However, in order to experience the quality of the fishing, certain techniques and approaches must be adhered to. I have lost count of the number of instances where I have encountered disillusioned Englishmen cursing a supposedly 'fishless' loch having endured an unsuccessful day afloat, hindered by the deployment of totally unsuitable fly fishing methods. Some do get it right, I hasten to add, and happier, more satisfied men you are unlikely to meet.

Locating Loch Trout

Those who enjoy success on large Scottish brown trout lochs do so by following a few simple, but golden rules. Before I outline them, one under-

Scenic splendour.

lying aspect must be considered: local knowledge. The benefits of attaining local knowledge are universally recognized by all anglers in every country, but in Scotland, due to the vast scale of many of the brownie waters, local knowledge can be especially beneficial. Often such knowledge can contradict what one has read or been told previously by those supposedly 'in the know'. That is why I stress that local advice should take precedence over all other recommendations. Adherence to the aforementioned 'golden rules' should see you through most circumstances, but if local knowledge is available – even if it is contradictory to what you already believe – then take it. Such information is worth its weight in gold – or fish, depending which you value most.

'Daunting', 'overwhelming' and 'intimidating' are adjectives most frequently used by visiting anglers to describe the massive lochs which confront them in Scotland. Vast, deep, dark and windswept waters await those who wish to explore the largest Scottish trout lochs. No undulating, fertile surrounding landscapes to be found here: jagged-edged mountain ridges largely provide the only focal point in an otherwise featureless terrain. Likewise, the water mass may offer no immediate visual clues as to where the fisherman is most likely to encounter *Salmo trutta fario*. However, there is no need to let the awesome prospect of dealing with such a water drive you to the nearest rainbow fishery; fortunately, 90 per cent of the water's surface can be largely ignored. A boat is really essential if you are to fish these larger waters thoroughly. Fish can, and have, been caught from the shoreline, but on such a sizeable area of water the walk from one shoreline to another if the fish are not forthcoming can be extremely arduous, even impossible. If your chosen loch has no boats advertised specifically for fishing, it is always worth making a few tentative enquiries to those with private boats on the loch. Co-operation and kindness are usually guaranteed. Reciprocation with a gesture of thanks is appreciated, and can greatly help your cause if a second visit is planned.

When and Where to Fish

The best time to fish the larger Scottish trout lochs – indeed, almost any Scottish loch – is between late April and early August. The peak months are, not surprisingly, May and June, with July not far behind, providing the weather is mild and wet. Sun-soaked 'dog-days' are not very productive, but if you confine your activities to the evenings, the fish will usually oblige. For the enthusiast, night fishing with dry sedges can provide some great sport; as the last glow of light fades from the west, some surprisingly large brownies can be caught only inches from the bank. However, it is daytime boat fishing that the visiting angler is most likely to choose, so it is this type of fly fishing on which I shall elaborate.

Your boat should be positioned over water which is between 8in (20cm) and 15ft (4½m) deep. The shallower water may be increasingly productive as evening progresses. 'If you can't see the bottom, then you're fishing too deep,' is an old adage and should, on the whole, be followed. On the larger Scottish lochs this means you should be fishing close to the shore. The gradient of the drop-off from shallow to deep water will vary with the loch: on some lochs such as Quoich and Clunie, the drop-off may be found as close as 2 to 3 feet (½ to 1m) from the shore, whereas on Rannoch, for example, the slope will be more gentle, with deep water being found some 20 yards (18m) out from the shore. Position your boat accordingly, though it is as well to remember that many Scottish waters are very peat-stained, so the bottom may not be visible much below 2½ to 3ft (½ to 1m). Shallow water may be the more productive if you are fishing early or late in the season, provided you fish a sinking line.

As the water warms during the course of the year, concentrate your efforts further from the shore – but not deeper than the 15 foot (4½m) mark. For spring and summer fishing (May to August) I personally like to be fishing in water around 3 to 10 feet (1 to 3m) deep. No matter what time of year you choose to fish, always pay particular attention to features such as islands, burn mouths and headlands. Many lochs are littered with inviting, intimate bays which also present a great chance of a fish or two! Flooded river mouths are particularly productive, though if the weather is very bright and sunny, fish around the deeper end of the scale; I have seldom caught trout in very shallow water on a sunny day. The brassy glare which can be uncomfortable on human eyes is, I believe, equally unappreciated by the brown trout, perhaps because it doesn't have eyelids. Thus the trout residing in very

Some marvellous fish fall as the water warms.

shallow water which is highly penetrable to the sun's rays has two choices: he can either spend the day sulking on the bottom, or he can head for the cover of slightly deeper water where he will continue to feed. Such a fish can still be caught on a floating line, however. The presentation of a moving fly in the water's surface may bring a reaction from the trout, who is still quite prepared to look up in the water for his next meal, despite spending his day a few feet below the surface.

Tactics and Tackle

When fishing for wild brownies on bright days, I have noticed that, whilst fishing with a floater will often move or rise more fish, sinking line tactics will actually put more fish in the boat. Why this should be so is unclear to me, but I can only think that such bright, brassy conditions affect the trout's vision. Perhaps also the trout intends to 'drown' the fly that is in the surface film, preferring to devour its meal away from the brightness,

somewhere under the surface. Thus the conclusions which govern line choice on a bright, cloudless, day remain dependent on individual choice and personal belief. However, I would advocate the use of a slow-sinking or Wet Cel 2 line on such a day.

With any luck, the visiting angler will not be presented with such sun-soaked conditions. Ideal conditions are more or less similar to those which might be wished for on any other fly-fishing loch in Britain, although a fiercer wind than would be desirable on English reservoirs does appear to bring out the best in Scottish brownies. Virtually no day is too windy for fish to be caught on the surface; it is only the launching of the boat which poses a restriction to the day's proceedings.

When chasing wild brownies, size of fly is as important as choice of fly, and perhaps even more so. For early and late season fishing, sizes 10 and 12 should suffice; during the less cold months, 12s and 14s should see you through most

What a fish! A wild brownie at its best.

eventualities; though bushy, palmered flies on a size 10 hook should be kept close by for use on the top dropper ('bob' position) during windy conditions. A minimal selection of very small dry flies and size 8 or 10 lures should also be carried in case a flat calm awaits. I am amazed at the frequency of such conditions on the very large Scottish lochs. Although the visitor would be unlucky to witness his chosen loch in such a 'mirror' state, flat calms are not an altogether irregular occurrence. If you cannot drive or walk over a hill to another loch where the wind is blowing (economy of effort is a Scottish trademark), then your best bet would be to deploy a fast sinking line and small lures. Nine times out of ten this technique will out-score dry fly fishing to individual rising trout.

As regards pattern of fly, and it has been said a million times, sticking to standard Scottish fly patterns will seldom send you home fishless. Within this category I would include the following: Bilbio, Black Pennell, Butchers, Invicta, Dunkeld, Blae 'n' Black, March Brown, Peter Ross and Zulus; the list is fairly sizeable. However, technique and flies which are the norm on most English reservoirs are not productive for Scotland's wild brownies; thus twitching a team of three buzzers, drifting emergers and dries, 'figure-of-eighting' nymphs or booby diving will not catch you many fish.

I have found that worrying about the specific pattern of fly to be fished is one of the least important aspects of Scottish wild brownie hunting; size of fly, as already mentioned is probably more significant. Speed of retrieve, however, is unquestionably crucial. One elderly individual whom it is my great pleasure to know, frequently curses his own increasing inability to retrieve his flies at the hectic pace he so favours. Very few anglers can claim to have caught as many wild brownies as this gentleman: his motto is 'You canny bring yer flees back tae quick fur oor broonies,' and generally I have found it to be good and true. Only in the coldest of conditions should your retrieve be slow and deliberate; early season, sunk-line work on the larger glacial lochs often demands such tactics. For all other occasions, keep the retrieve fast and erratic.

Whether hungry or not, the sudden appearance of a fly flashing through a brown trout's territory will provoke from it an instinctive reaction. As many anglers know, takes are often incredibly fast, so timing of the strike should be surgical. On days when the fish rise and thrash endlessly at the flies without actually taking a firm hold, try a smaller size of the same pattern of fly. Alternatively, once a fish has splashed at your fly, do not strike but leave the fly static for about ten seconds. Often the fish will try to drown the fly before a more decisive take occurs.

Many Scottish anglers when fishing for wild brownies cast a four-fly leader, yet no angler I have ever met has been able to provide me with visual evidence that four flies are better than three. The only statistic that is likely to increase if you opt for a four fly cast is that relating to the number of leader tangles you will experience. Fishing four flies has no clear advantage unless you wish to establish which fly a localized rise of fish is preoccupied with.

In order to catch fish constantly on a three-fly cast, it is imperative that your top dropper fly is sufficiently bushy to create a surface wake when fished on a floating line. Even when fishing a sinker, the bob fly should make a sizeable commotion when emerging from the water's surface in front of the boat. If a sinking line is your first choice, always remember to 'hang' the flies in the water at the end of the retrieve; on some days this is the only way to induce a trout to take. If a floater is deployed, try to ensure your bob fly makes as big as fuss as possible on the surface of the water, and 'dibble' that bob fly close to the boat at the end of the retrieve. Then watch out for fast takes! When using a floater or an intermediate, the rod should be raised slowly to the vertical position during the course of the retrieve. Not so for sunken lines. Wild brownies can take and reject flies underwater so fast that 'takes' may not even register. For best chance of contact, keep the rod tip near the water's surface; do not allow a loop of line to appear at the end of your rod, and keep well in touch with your flies at all times.

As regards leader construction, double-strength nylon is not necessary. A 13ft leader of 4lb Maxima or Drennan, straight through, is all that is required if your plan of attack is to fish in a 'traditional' loch-style manner. Step up to 5lb or 6lb if using a Wet Cel 2 or Hi-D; rarely should you need to go beyond this. In order to avoid confusion it is worth familiarizing yourself with Scots fly-fishing vocabulary at this stage. The top dropper position (nearest the fly line) is referred to as the 'bob'; the name hints at the very purpose of this position on the leader. That which is commonly referred to as the 'point' position by most other British anglers is termed the 'tail' position by Scots. Most Scottish anglers use 12 to 14ft leaders on floating lines: 6 or 7ft to the 'bob', 3½ to the middle fly and 3 feet to the tail. Leaders which taper from 6 to 4lb accentuate presentation, which can be helpful on very clear waters, as clumsy casting can easily spook fish. For sunk-line work, leaders should be shortened slightly, but always keep a minimum of 3½ft between flies.

Fishing by Boat

Ninety-nine per cent of wild brownie fishing is by drifting. Anchoring in order to fish from a static boat is extremely rare, and unheard of on most lochs; long, lingering drifts are sought. A drogue is an essential item for Scottish loch fishing. Three anglers per boat is the norm, with only two actually fishing at any one time; this allows a half-hourly rotation of oarwork. Such a system of 'two fishing, one on the oars' allows the boat to be held securely on the chosen drift. If this is not necessary, the man in the middle – if his partners agree

– can very delicately fish a short line close to the boat. Brushing the water's surface with wake-producing flies can be highly effective, helping to hold the interest of the fish near to the boat and thus benefiting the other two rods. It is not without reason that traditionally, gillies used dapping methods from the middle seat, in order to pull up fish for their clients.

Those who have fished in Scotland for brownies on a semi-regular basis will know that the most prolific times are during spring and summer. For reasons best known to themselves, wild brownies respond better to flies fished on or very near the surface; even the best of Scottish fly fishers seldom experience bonanzas when fishing sinking lines. Why sunk tactics should not fare so well is unknown; perhaps these trout are simply less inclined to grab a sunken fly than their trans-atlantic cousins.

For me, boat position and location is the single most important component when hunting wild browns on Scottish lochs: master this aspect and you have every likelihood of success. As all good fly fishers know, it pays to be adaptable, but when fishing in Scotland never ignore 'traditional'

Two huge fish, but rather lean at the beginning of the year.

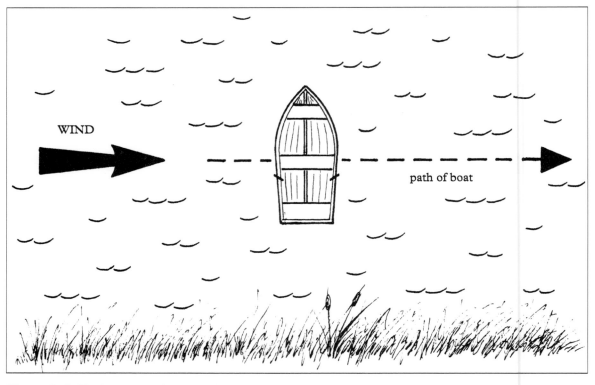

Fig. 28 *Probably the most usual way of fishing the lochs (or any big stillwater for that matter) is by boat. The boat is positioned across the wind and it will travel along the shore, following that important drop-off for many yards or even miles if the conditions are right. It is possible for two people to fish quite happily like this, but if conditions are tricky the man on the oars can rectify the drift as need be.*

methods – their very existence is proof that certain techniques have stood the test of time. Crudely basic? Maybe. Productive? Definitely. Remember also that with the choice of lochs Scotland has to offer, don't just stick to one water if the fish are not co-operative: explore and enjoy.

Safety First

A final word of warning: the speed with which pleasant weather can become hideous and highly dangerous on large Scottish lochs has to be seen to be believed. When you set out, take warm waterproof clothing with you, no matter how subdued the weather appears; and if things get dangerous, get to the nearest shore. No fish that swims is worth risking your life for, so don't try to get back to 'base' if danger threatens. Posthumous medals for bravery will not be distributed.

These basic methods I have outlined should

see you through most eventualities. 'Golden rules' are fundamentally helpful, but bear in mind the benefits of 'here and now' local advice. Together, you should have all the information you need to spend a wonderful day afloat, with a basketful of golden-bellied wild brownies to show at the end of the day.

Go thou and do likewise.

Postscript

At a later date I was asked again why and how the question of light affects the fish. This question is particularly pertinent to fishing Scottish waters, so I am happy to elaborate. First of all, the weak rays of the sun at the beginning and the end of the season are only capable of penetrating the very shallowest of water. As a result, insect activity is at its greatest in this depth of water. Also, high rainfall on many Scottish lochs at these times of

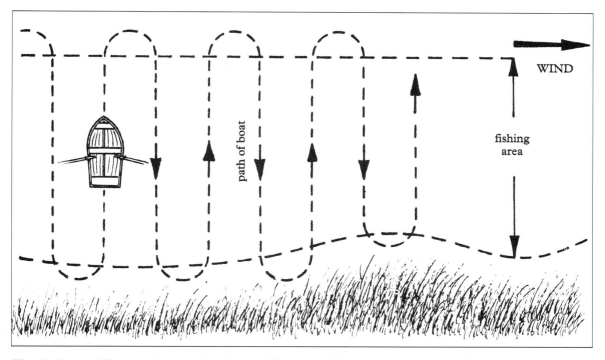

Fig. 29 *Once a killing area has been found it is possible to extend the amount of water fished by moving backwards and forwards across the taking zone. Of course, this does require one man to be constantly on the oars.*

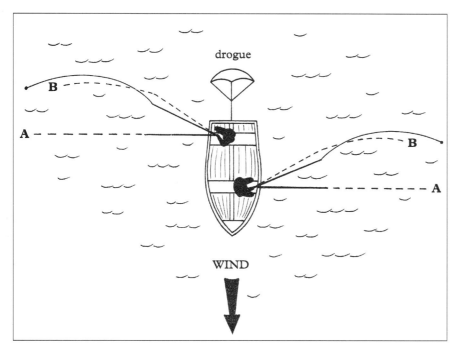

Fig. 30 *A common practise on any large water these days is the use of the drogue. This slows the boat's progress down the wind lanes and allows two anglers to fish a prime water in relative ease and with great efficiency.*

the year can also raise water levels quite dramatically, unless they've been used for hydro-electric power schemes, of course.

As the water rises, burn mouths, grassland and shorelines all become flooded. These areas provide a haven for insects, and the trout won't waste any time in venturing over them. On the bigger Scottish lochs nearly all my early season work is done on these areas, and they *always* hold fish. Once the sun gets stronger and the deeper water becomes warmer, then the trout move out from the shoreline a fair bit, so it is quite critical to get the depth of water right – too deep early on and there won't be any insect life, and too shallow later on and the brightness might be too great.

What I have said about catching trout in shallow water on sunny days may be open to criticism, and so it should be. After all, this is only my personal theory and such a thing will always be questioned; but I do know for sure that I have seldom caught brownies in shallow water during very bright conditions. The brightness of the day seems to be critical.

Can I repeat here that I honestly believe the actual fly pattern is far less important than most people believe. When pulling flies through the waves as fast as most Scots do for browns, does it really make any sense to argue that a lighter shade of hen hackle or a thicker wing of teal will make the difference between fish and no fish? I certainly have my doubts on the usefulness of 'variants' which are always – and will always be – created in ever-increasing numbers. What's that old saying about flies catching anglers and not the fish?

I'd also like to say just a little bit more about lines. Honestly, there is no such thing as a day that is too windy to catch wild browns. Fishing an intermediate line can let your flies fish through the waves more shortly, giving the trout a better sight of the flies. What I cannot really comprehend is why wild browns will not co-operate when sinking lines are used; I've never done very well when forced to fish deeper than an intermediate for browns. I should, however, make a distinction here between wild and stocked fish: I've had good bags of stocked browns on sinking tactics, but not so with wildies. Why? I really don't know the answer to that one; anything more than a double brace on a sunk line and you have done very well indeed. So, I wonder if anyone can shed light onto that one? I have one or two little theories, but nothing concrete.

A DAY ON LOCH LOCHY

Lochy is a daunting water, several miles long, on average a mile wide and, in places, frighteningly deep. It is part of the Great Glen system and moves into Loch Oich and from there into Ness itself. All in all we are looking at over thirty miles length of water, averaging a mile in width and often approaching 1,000ft deep. The volume alone is a daunting proposition: how on earth do you get a trout to find a single artificial fly, or even a team, in such an ocean?

Although I have frequently trolled Lochy in the past, this was my first attempt on it with the fly. It was the end of the season, and September had hustled in some unsettled weather; the nights were getting colder, and the rain occasionally had the sting and feel of sleet. But at least there was some breeze and low cloud cover, and that gave Gordon Heath, my partner for the day, a certain amount of heart.

We put the boat in at the Oich end of the loch. Overnight a slight easterly breeze had set in and this at least kept the rain off. Weak though the wind was, there was enough chop for a drift and we had some hope of success even though conditions were far from ideal.

We both put simple 9½ft rods, using floating lines and teams of three flies. I noticed that Gordon made a very traditional selection, while I went for one of the newer Gold Head nymphs on the tail to try and give that little bit of extra weight so that the flies would be spaced out nicely throughout the water – at least, that was my idea.

Gordon had heard that there were some good rainbow trout – long-term escapees from a trout farm – that had taken up residence on the north shore, along a slightly shallower, sandy and rocky bank in the vicinity of a line of trees. We motored three-quarters of the way across before switching off the engine, manoeuvering the boat to the head of the drift, and then letting that easterly wind push us slowly down, broadside, until we were about thirty yards from the bank.

This is traditional loch-style fishing: the boat moves slowly through a prime area, and you are constantly approaching undisturbed water and

A dour day on Loch Oich.

unaware fish. Gordon was quite adamant about the distance to be kept from the bank, and each time we strayed out a little into deeper water he would pull a couple of times on the oars to bring us back into casting range of the shore. I noticed that he kept looking over the side of the boat watching for the bottom to appear again from the depths. This is the killing zone, that crucial drop-off from shallow to deep water which trout love to patrol.

Though Gordon and I had not fly fished together, loch-style, for some while, we soon settled into an easy casting procedure, working our flies back to the boat fractionally out of time so that only one of us was casting at once. We were both casting a reasonable length of line, around 15m or so. There are some skilled loch fishers who like to use shorter line and keep the flies working more busily; however, it was very clear water, and we tended to think that the trout would feed more confidently further away from

the boat – but obviously conditions play their part as well as simple theory.

The retrieves were critical, we found that day. Gordon was working his flies quite a bit faster than mine; often I was making only one cast to his two, but that seemed to work for him and all in all, through the course of the day, he probably had three offers to every two of mine, even though we swapped flies consistently. Of particular importance seemed to be the dibble at the end of the retrieve just before the lift-off for the next cast, and Gordon registered more takes throughout the day at this crucial stage than at any other time through the retrieve. Obviously fish were following the flies in, showing interest, but only being provoked into some sort of action at the end with the traditional induced take. On certain drifts, four or five fish might show interest right at this final stage, generally to the bob fly as it danced on the surface or even fractionally above.

The boat drifts down parallel to the shore along the drop-off.

In the first part of the morning we managed a few rainbows, all well hooked, very well mended after their stew-pond start to life and supremely fit. All in all we felt that things looked set for a pleasant bit of fishing. Then the wind died completely, eddied about a bit, scratching its head, and finally decided to come in from the west. Suddenly the cloud that had kept above the Munroes dropped, and swathed them in mist; first of all we were hit by drizzle, and soon a steady, cold soaking rain. The wind then strengthened so much that we considered putting a drogue out to slow our drift down, but eventually it dropped considerably and we found there was no need.

Suddenly, and I mean suddenly, the trout began to come short to the flies; Gordon felt at least a dozen takes, and myself about seven or eight, though with no fish properly hooked. It was all a bit baffling; my own feeling is that a drop in pressure, especially a sudden one, has a dramatic

effect on the feeding behaviour of fish, and not just trout but all freshwater fish in general. Time and again throughout my fishing career I have noticed that very often fish can actually sense the approach of falling pressure, many hours before the barometer even begins to move. My own feeling that afternoon was that this explained exactly the behaviour of these trout: they were still moving, still interested to a certain extent, but not really committing themselves – hence the endless succession of tugs and boils at the fly.

By now the autumn afternoon was becoming fairly weary. We rode past a point on the loch towards a large shallow bay; a couple of Central Belters were holding fort there, fishermen from the Glasgow area, sitting by a fire, bait rods propped up against a pile of stones, watching indicators as their worms lay unmoving on the bottom. In the trees behind them hung several polythene bags, all bulging with trout. It is not really for me, an Englishman, to make any comment on this systematic rape of the Highlands by the bottom fishermen from Glasgow; I suppose it is only right and fine that city Scots should be able to get out at the weekend and enjoy the glories of their country. But it does seem a shame – and I am certainly backed up in this by nearly every Highland fisherman I know – that all the fish that they catch, no matter how small, have to end up in a bag swinging from a tree. I suppose if they are set on using worms and on fishing like this, there isn't much we can do, even though it is against the law; but surely small fish that *can* be returned, *should* be, for the good of fishing in the future.

We had high hopes initially of some sport in this large shallow bay, at least eighty or ninety acres with weed showing here and there. However, we were to be disappointed: although we

Success! Joy holds a small fish taken on the point fly.

rowed and drifted and fished for an hour and a half, we did not get a single tug. The wind was getting keener all the time, and the rain colder and no doubt the temperature was dropping fast; perhaps that was enough to put an end to sport for the day. Gordon, however, true trout fisherman that he is, blamed the number of jack pike in that particular area of Lochy. His own feeling is that the number of pike in the shallow weeded areas of the loch acts as a natural deterrent to trout coming in to investigate and to feed. Perhaps he is right: my own worry is that trout anglers kill *all* pike, not just the small ones. I agree that small pike, say under 12 or 15lb, must be removed, but if we take away the large ones that feed almost exclusively on small pike, then population explosions of pike are bound to occur.

At about six o'clock we decided we had had enough, and rowed for the shore. Loch-style fishing like this is a lovely way to take trout. It is a real pleasure to be afloat on a beautiful water on a pleasant day, feeling yourself being gently pushed through prime areas by a helpful wind. You soon get into the rhythm of things, concentrating on the fishing, feeling a lurch of excitement at every pull but still being able to relax, to settle back into that easy comradeship which is so easy to pick up again, even after a matter of years, if you are a true fisherman. And always at the back of your mind is the thought of a possible big fish. Every year trout well over 4lb fall to anglers drifting and fishing carefully with the right flies. It is tempting to think that large Scottish or Irish trout only come on the troll, but this is not the case at all. I have heard of many fish up just over 11lb that have come on flies no bigger than a 14. And what an achievement and what a fight such a combination represents.

LOCHAN FISHING

The Welsh hills to an extent, and the Scottish mountains in particular, offer some of the most spectacular stillwater fly fishing in Europe. At high altitude, in remote places, it is possible to find waters that have never been fished or at least for which no records exist. This fact alone makes fishing such places – often tiny and always rugged – exciting, but the fishing is also frequently profitable. After all, none of these waters suffer from the typical angling pressure of the modern age, and only otters, pine martens, cormorants and ospreys serve to keep down the numbers of wild fish

Numbers, in fact, are often the main problem on lochans: at altitude, feeding is often poor; springs are slow and autumns early, and with few predators, the waters are often vastly over-stocked with six, eight or even ten fish to the pound. Such tiny fish can be disappointing if you have made a five-hour climb through mist and rain, and it is tempting to write the water off for your lifetime – but this would be a mistake. Any situation can change: a few cormorants can thin fish out dramatically and within two years the survivors might well be into the 4 to 6oz (120 to 170g) range and growing steadily. So it never pays to discount these small, unknown waters completely, and it is wise to cast an eye on them, even the most unpromising ones, every five years or so.

Just a handful of lochans have brought me the most pleasure over the years. Let me start with a three-acre lochan perched beneath Gairich, a Munroe in Knoydart. I'd often fished the major loch beneath, and would sometimes pull the boat into the southern shore and climb to the summit of Gairich to take in the entirety of this beautiful environment. On several occasions I'd passed the lochan, hardly bothering to give it a second look, until on one of my trips to 3000ft (900m) I noticed a pair of shags working constantly, obviously catching fish. I was intrigued. According to all the information I could find, nobody ever fished the water or even dreamt that at 2000ft (600m) there would be fish present; but obviously there were, and the next day I was up there with a fly rod to find out.

I can't say that the sport was fast and furious, but two hours' fishing brought me seven or eight pulls and five fish on the bank, all extraordinarily coloured and shaped and in perfect condition. All were like peas in a pod, about 8oz and fought magnificently. The great satisfaction of this particular day was knowing that almost certainly I was the first to fish this water for many years – possibly the first ever – and the excitement of catching totally virgin fish in such a spectacular setting has stayed with me ever since.

Lochan trout are often five or even six to the pound, though sometimes they are bigger. They are almost always splendid to look at.

My lochan fishing goes back much further than this, to a particular summer in the late seventies in north Wales when I set out to look for three lakes I had been told about, miles from civilization. Eventually I did find them, beautiful in their isolation, and began to fish with excitement. The first lake was extraordinary, about two acres in extent but I doubt more than two feet(½m) deep anywhere – take the fish out and I think it would only have been six inches (15cm) in depth! These fish were remarkable: there were literally thousands of miniature trout, most of them no larger than minnows or gudgeon; I drifted out a little bit of floating tissue and it was pulled to bits within two yards by hordes of ravening fish. It was impossible to cast anywhere without getting tugs immediately, although most of the fish were too small to take in even a size 16 hook successfully. Nevertheless these minuscule trout were just as beautiful as any I have ever seen.

At the second of the lakes I fished hard for two hours but without a pull at all, so then I moved to the third. This was it: within an hour I had landed four fish, one of a quite stunning 1lb 10oz – big, deep, broad, dark and dashingly spotted. Over the following three years I made an annual pilgrimage to these three remote waters, never failing to find some extraordinary fish, but always coming away blank from that second, mysterious water where I never saw a single fish rise.

Recently I ran into Christopher in the north of Scotland, quite ecstatic after a holiday in a cottage in Sutherland, apparently surrounded by waters and where the fishing was marvellous. He had used the lightest of gear throughout, just a brook rod, and casting with no more than a 1½lb breaking strain. Most of the fish came to dry flies, tiny ones tied on a size 18 or even a 20, and dusk was evidently the killing time; but during the day, small nymphs fished in and around the bottom

This is the water situated at around 1,200ft (365m), full of small fish.

weed proved just as successful. Never once in the entire week did he see another soul and it was as though the whole world belonged to him and his spaniel, Maddy. But it was the quality of the fishing that was so amazing: his biggest trout weighed in at over 4lb and in the course of that week he had another thirty of over 2lb, all taken on this fragile tackle, and some after fights that he described as the most memorable of his life – and this from a man who has landed many a Tay salmon! Obviously the key to all this magic was remoteness: perhaps ten or fifteen anglers a year managed to fish these jewels.

The size of some of these high-altitude lochans never ceases to amaze. The Clunie Ridge stretches proud and unbroken for several miles, and on its south side, at the foot of a scree, lies a small water of about 1½ acres (¾ha) in extent. Again we are talking about another water at 2,300ft (700m) at least, surrounded by rocks, blasted by gales, and altogether as inhospitable an environment for trout as one would think possible; and yet on a clear, bright May day I looked down on it through binoculars and saw big fish patrolling the shallows. Two days later I was back with climbing boots and rod, sliding down the scree, creeping along the barren bank, working a team of flies. Just two fish fell that day, one over 1½lb and the larger a fraction under 2lb. Was I the first to fish that lochan in that wild place? Can I be the only one to have seen such extraordinary fish leap from such an amazing water?

I remember a group of five lochans in Westeross, eight miles from the nearest road and involving a very long trudge across damp moorland. Yet that journey would always be worthwhile, always well rewarded by the wildlife, the beautiful loneliness and the guaranteed, super bags of anything between twenty and forty trout averaging ½lb or more. I mention these lakes because amongst all these small fish, very occasionally a really large one takes you by surprise. On two or three occasions I have been taken and then really put to the test by a trout well over 3lb, just odd fish amongst three or four hundred ordinary ones, but they still come along, out of the blue, preventing any smugness or lack of concentration.

I could go on recounting tales of over ninety small hill waters that I have fished over the years, some holding char, some holding big trout, one holding a surprise stock of rainbows, and all capable of producing the most extraordinary fishing – and I am not even an expert or a real explorer. There are people who make lochan fishing the central point of their fly fishing lives, and goodness knows what stories they would have to tell. But the main point is that here there is fabulous fishing, and generally for free, for anybody prepared to walk, and occasionally rough it in grim weather.

Tackle and Equipment

It is always wise to travel light when walking these long distances, and the amount of tackle that needs to be taken is minimal: a rod, a reel, a floating line, casts down to as low as 2lb at the point and a tin of general flies; I wouldn't even bother with a landing net these days. Keep it as simple as you like and you will catch fish almost certainly: after all, these are not sophisticated, hard-fished trout – it is getting to them that is the achievement!

Remember that you will be doing a lot of walking, both to get there and probably when you arrive at the water, so think carefully about your clothing. You want to be able to walk freely, without perspiring unduly, and yet you will need to keep warm if the weather comes in wet and cold. Wellingtons will almost certainly be necessary for when you arrive at the water, though perhaps light thigh-boots will do best. I am not a hat person but even so, I am never tempted to go out to 2,000ft (600m) without some sort of head gear, as the weather can change dramatically. It is also advisable to take some food and perhaps a small flask. A lot of these lochans involve a strenuous climb and often a round trip of ten or even fifteen miles (16 to 24km), so you will be a whole day away from base. You can do this without food, but it makes sense to refuel as you go.

Safety Precautions

In Wales, and in Scotland particularly, the weather is fickle and can and does change dramatically: therefore it is *always* wise to get as detailed a weather report as you can before

A typical lochan trout, but just look at the weather: rain streaming in from the west. It never does to take these far-flung waters anything less than seriously.

making up your mind about a day out on the remote hills. Because of the rough terrain, accurate weather reports are often difficult to get, but it pays to make a sensible decision based on every scrap of advice that you can obtain.

Never take safety for granted when you are fishing these remote areas. Be sure to take a detailed map of the expedition area: this is vital, both to find your way to the water and to return home again. A compass is just as essential as the map, and make sure that you know how to use

both in conjunction. There are also some excellent books on general hill walking, and these should be read, and the techniques practised. A pair of light binoculars is useful, certainly for the pleasure of watching deer or the different bird species, but also, in extremes, for safety: there are times when you really do need as clear a view of your surroundings as possible.

Never neglect to tell people back at base where you aim to be going; if you are long overdue, then at least they will be able to launch a search party in roughly the right direction. It is always tempting to push off quietly on your own to do a little bit of exploring with your trout rod, but do remember these can be wild, unforgiving places for the unwary.

Manners and Etiquette

Finally, towards the end of the season, do be very careful that your wanderings in the hills are not going to upset the stalking activities on the local estates. Whether you agree with the moral principles of stalking or not, it is important to realize that deer, in the Highlands especially, do need to be culled on an annual basis, and stalking is probably the only practical and humane way of doing this. Remember that stalking does serve a crucial economic function in the Highlands, employing many people annually. Nearly all the estate owners throw open their hills to general walkers most of the year round, and it is only fair to respect their limited demands in this important season for them.

Remember, too, that the fishing will nearly always be free to anybody who makes the effort to get there, but it is only polite to make sure that it *is* allowed. You can check at local hotels, inns, with the stalkers or even ring the estate offices; it is rare that a civilized request will be refused.

I have concentrated on these lochans because I really do feel there is the most dramatic, free, lovely fishing available which is untouched by or hardly even recognized by the general angler. Most will flock along the well-trodden paths to the stillwaters everyone knows about, quite ignoring the fact that here are many other jewels, sprinkled over the mountains by the liberal hands of our fishing gods.

11 FEROX TROUT

Ferox trout might not yet be regarded as a mainstream species for the trout fisherman, but they once were: the Victorians and the Edwardians had the sense to realize that the ferox was probably one of the most sporting fish available in the British Isles. From 1850 a succession of English anglers travelled to Scotland in search of ferox trout and frequently were highly successful; their stories percolated British angling literature for at least eighty or ninety years, until the ferox scene went quiet. This was easy to understand: ferox trout are not easy to catch, and large amounts of time, effort and money were needed even before one came grudgingly to the net. Time and money were of no great consequence in certain echelons of society before the Second World War, and the ferox trout quest could quite justifiably be fitted into the Scottish season enjoyed by the upper

A huge ferox trout: the one-time record of 19lb 9oz caught from Loch Quoich. The fish is held by that excellent ferox man, John Hett (left) and the hotel proprietor and fisherman of renown, Gordon Heath.

middle class or the aristocracy. But things changed after 1945 when a new mood of austerity and work-consciousness settled on all classes; no longer could many sportsmen enjoy the luxury of vast amounts of time simply spent fishing. So the ferox trout began to disappear from the angling mind, and the truth about this extraordinary fish became clouded.

In the 1950s a myth began to grow that ferox trout were simply predatorial fish grown big-headed, ugly and thin-bodied, almost invariably going back in condition, on the point of death. Book after book proclaimed this fatuous thesis, probably as a way to avoid the subject. Certainly when I began to fish seriously for ferox trout in the early 1980s, it was difficult to find anybody with anything good to say about the fish at all – even though most anglers had never laid eyes on a ferox or hardly knew what one was. Even today despite the strenuous efforts of myself and groups such as the Ferox '85 Club there are many anglers who are still mystified when it comes to the subject of ferox trout. So what is a ferox?

The Victorians maintained that the ferox was a distinct sub-species of trout, and not simply an ordinary trout that had mysteriously grown large; though of course, the Victorians were very keen on proving that the fish world was populated with far more species and sub-species than had ever been thought of before. This belief in the sub-species philosophy was ridiculed after the Second World War, again by scientists and anglers who knew very little about ferox and showed no inclination to learn. Thus from 1950 the ferox was seen as nothing more than a large brown trout that had happened to turn predatorial and was in no way particularly special. It was only during the 1980s that the pendulum swung back again and the ferox was once again recognized as a distinct sub-species.

Now, there seems no doubt whatsoever that the ferox is a fish apart from the normal brown trout. For example in Scotland, the normal brownie grows for about three or four years, holds its condition and weight for a year or so, and then dies at about six years of age. The ferox is quite different: it actually grows for twelve to fourteen years,

MAJOR-GENERAL SIR WILFRID MALLESON, HIS RECORD TROUT (17 lb, 2 oz.), AND PILZ

Big ferox have always been prized both here and on the Continent. This is a massive Alpine fish.

with an accelerating period between six and eight years – the very moment when most brown trout are dying. After this growth period stops, the ferox probably holds its condition for another two or three years before dying perhaps aged eighteen to twenty. Obviously the longevity of the ferox has a great deal to do with their size and their ability to take fish as food from quite an early age, say around two or three years.

Research has proved that ferox only breed with other ferox in the autumn at certain specialized sites. This means that the sub-species remains intact, and ferox strains continue to prosper in the large lochs. The ferox is, of course, a fish of the largest waters in the United Kingdom and abroad. This is because the ferox strain of trout is directly related to the existence of char populations as regards growth and development. Char are the key: char colonized the large glacial lakes of Scotland and to an extent the Lake District and parts of Ireland, and it was these huge char populations that enabled the ferox to develop. Trout, even big trout, are not superbly equipped predators like pike: their mouths are really too small and their head is the wrong shape, which means they find it very difficult to prey successfully on individual fish; they need a big shoal to lunge into if they are going to hunt successfully. Small brown trout do not group in this manner, and if char did not exist, then neither would ferox. It is as well that the char populations in many prolific lochs number millions, for without them we would be denied these extraordinary, colossal brown trout.

The link between char and ferox trout has been recognized now for nearly twenty years and it is a very strong bond indeed, in fact, ferox trout probably do not exist where char are absent, except perhaps in rare circumstances such as Loch Lomond where powan might have taken the place of char as a food supply. In general terms, however, you have to look at the Irish loughs such as Mask, the English lakes such as Windermere and the Scottish lochs such as Awe to find ferox trout. Abroad, the large lakes of southern Germany, Austria, northern Italy, Switzerland and parts of France also appear to offer ferox possibilities, perhaps on an even mightier scale than we can hope for in Scotland. Indeed, my researches into the European glacial lakes seem to suggest that ferox in these waters can easily top 40lb and perhaps even a good deal more. In Scotland a 7lb ferox is a good fish, a ten-pounder a superb fish, a fifteen-pounder a fish of a lifetime and a twenty-pounder a record. However, that does not mean necessarily that bigger ferox do not exist.

It is quite wicked that the one-time British record brown trout of 39½lb was discounted. This fish was taken in Loch Awe in the 1880s, displayed for two or three days to all and sundry, then sent to a top taxidermist and set up in a case. The Victorians knew what they were talking about, and if so many people witnessed its capture and identification there seems little doubt to me, at least, that the fish was a trout and not, as it has now been said, a kelt. That, to me again, is palpably nonsense; the Victorians were excellent at fish biology, and why should so many experts have made such an obvious mistake?

This belief is backed up by the fact that at least two 30lb trout have been taken recently from Loch Awe in fish nets laid by research teams. Today's scientists have verified both of these fish as trout, and there is now no denying that ferox can easily top 30lb in weight, and perhaps even nudge towards 40lb. Imagine it! A 40lb wild ferox trout from one of the most beautiful waters imaginable. Obviously, most of us have to fish for ordinary trout in typical waters most of our angling lives, but there is no reason why we cannot dream or perhaps devote some holiday time to the pursuit of these most fantastic of brown trout.

And what about this monster from the German Lakes?

FEROX TACKLE AND FISHING METHODS

Traditionally the ferox was fished for on the troll, using either an artificial or a natural bait, pulled behind the boat at great depth. It was probably this style of fishing that contributed to the decline in the popularity of the ferox as a target species. Writer after writer through the 1950s condemned this type of fishing as appallingly dull and mindless, and even today there are many trout anglers who would not consider trolling a bait. Fair enough. I can appreciate this point of view, and certainly of my hundreds of days on Scottish lochs very many have proved anything but dynamically interesting; I admit that when a harsh wind is blowing and there are snowflakes or sleet in the air and a ferox trout hasn't been seen for a week it is very difficult to keep going. However, trolling need not be like this. Modern equipment has made it much more interesting and satisfying and

it *can* be fun. Also, and this is the most important, there are other ways of catching ferox trout, some of which are as exciting as any imaginable.

Trolling for Ferox

Where do we start? Well, let's look at trolling. Obviously you need a boat and a good reliable engine that will tick over quite smoothly hour upon hour without oiling up. You also need a fair amount of skill as a boatman if you are going out alone and intend to control the boat and fish two rods by yourself. This is not so easy as it might seem, especially if a bit of a wind begins to blow up, or a fish is hooked, or you get into anything like a tangle. In the the past I have been wrapped up like a Christmas parcel, and the whole enterprise can become dangerous and embarrassing.

Rods and Reels for Trolling

Rods need to be about 9 to 10ft, and fairly soft-actioned; light carp or pike rods are ideal. At one

A typical ferox scene; a boat is essential.

time it was considered essential to have multiplier reels, but now that the baitrunner device has appeared on the angling scene the normal fixed-spool reel is quite adequate. Lines need to be about 10 to 12lb bs and should be checked regularly; I would recommend putting on about 80yd (73m) of new line every second or third day of fishing.

Plugs and Spinners

You also need a decent selection of plugs and spinners. It is very difficult indeed to offer real guidelines here, because so many lures will work once or twice but not on a regular basis, it seems. Broadly, choose plugs and spinners that are about 3 to 4in (7 to 10cm) long, of bright colour generally and have the ability to work deep – certainly at 20 to 30ft (6 to 9m). This opens up quite a range of artificial lures to you, especially now that American models are beginning to flood onto the market. There is at least one supplier that can now offer just about anything you might want, and I would suggest equipping yourself with a good selection of deep working artificials. Keep experimenting, keep thinking and keep your confidence high, and surely a ferox will come your way.

Baits

The other alternative is to use a small dead trout, char or even sea fish as a trolled deadbait. These can be set up on a trace with two or three trebles, and a couple of coffin-leads 6in (15cm) above them will take them down to the required depth. Moved steadily through the water, they twist and dart and gleam not unlike a real fish.

It is hard to be certain which is the most effective type of bait, the dead natural or the artificial. I have had fish on both, and my own preferences veer from one to the other. It's not a bad idea to fish one rod with an artificial and another with a natural and compare results, as I have done for about eleven years – though even at the end of all that time I still can't make my mind up! If you are going to use a natural bait, it does have to be fresh: it's no use having a couple of small brown trout and keeping them putrefying in the boat for a day or two before mounting them. If they were alive until immediately before fishing, then so much the better, and I cannot over-stress the importance of this in my experience.

Whether artificial or natural, the bait seems to be best fished between 50 and 80yd (45 and 73m) behind the boat. This is not an absolute rule, but I do have this feeling that ferox are aware of boats going overhead and tend to prefer lures that are well out of what they sense to be the danger zone. I used to think that a slow trolled bait was probably the best, but now I have revised my opinion on that point: it is probably best to fish at just under walking speed or even a little above. In the early nineties a great many ferox fell to small lures fished at around 5 or 6mph (8 or 9kph)! Apparently the fish came at them like bats out of hell, something never to be forgotten.

Rod-rests

It is now time to talk about two or three specialized and important pieces of equipment. The first of these is the boat rod-rest: you really do need a strong and stable rod-rest clamped to the side of the boat; this will look after at least one rod so you can hold the second rod with one hand and operate the engine with the other. It is also a good idea to tie a rope from your rod to a fixed point in the boat, as more than one rod and reel has disappeared into the depths – I lost two in one week! Do make sure that the boat rod-rest is attached as firmly as possible because it does take a great deal of buffeting, especially in high winds which are never far away in the far north.

Downriggers

The next bit of equipment is the downrigger, a device brought in from America which keeps the lures at a predetermined depth; this can be anything up to 100ft (30m) plus. I don't like them: I have used them on the Scottish lochs and feel they can be a menace. They depend on a very heavy cannonball weighing 3 to 4lb to keep the whole affair down, and the danger is that this can become trapped on the stony bottom of the loch. If this happens and there is a big swell on, you are in *real* trouble because the boat cannot escape and you run the risk of pulling the wire right off it. All you can do in these circumstances is to

An aerial view of Loch Quoich, one-time home of the record brown trout.

Two small-water browns taken in the spring-time.

Two excellent brown trout taken on dry fly. Dry fly fishing is frequently overlooked on the stillwater scene, and this is a mistake – especially in early morning and at dawn, when these fish fell.

A magnificent Irish ferox for Des Elliott.

A view of Mask as a storm approaches: one of the finest stillwater trout lakes in the world.

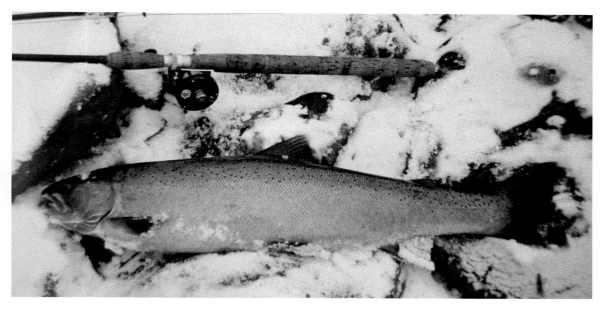

A sight we are unlikely ever to see in Britain: the steelhead. This North American sea-run rainbow trout is considered one of the greatest fighting fish in the world.

Nothing could be more exotic than the lenok trout that inhabits Siberia and Mongolia. This is very similar to our own rainbow, but the mouth is much more under-slung, like that of the barbel or mullet – presumably so it can scrape algae from the stones in hard winter weather.

The appeal of the western lakes is immense.

Fishing the lochans is a magnificent experience.

Teaching the young is a vital part of the angling process.

A lovely lake in the early summer.

Trout rearing-pens – the sign of a well-managed water.

Planning the day's strategy.

A glowing rainbow is the reward.

Never forget the basics on waters as big as these.

An echo-sounder of some sort is absolutely essential.

have the clippers handy and snip the wire that attaches to the trapped cannonball. In short, if you are out in a boat on your own, the down-rigger, in my experience, is an unnecessary and sometimes dangerous tool: always treat it with a certain amount of caution.

Fish-finders
This is not the case with the fish-finder, the electronic echo-sounder. My own machine is a portable Hummingbird which I have had for about eight trouble-free years. Being portable, I can move it from boat to boat, and it weighs no more than the average lady's handbag; the transducer simply sticks to the underneath of the boat and feeds the information back to the computer screen on the machine. Such information is always fascinating: not only do you get an instant

idea of the depth, but also of the bottom contours. You also see the fish – in Ireland I have actually caught a fish that I saw on the screen. In Scotland this has never been the case, in spite of all my hopes on the first trip: on such vast, deep, windswept waters it is quite impossible to spot a fish on the screen, moor up and attack it specifically; besides which you can never be sure that the big fish you think you see isn't a branch submerged at 20ft (6m) or more.

Basically, the fish-finder shows you the intimacies of the loch that you are fishing, and for that alone it is the greatest boon imaginable. In the heyday of ferox fishing, a hundred years back, you would hire a boatman week in, week out, who knew the water extremely well; however, this is not really an option today, hence the fish-finder and its central role.

The fish-finder has revealed a great deal about ferox and their behaviour. Certainly it picks out the huge char shoals that inhabit the big Scottish lochs, and in the early days especially it was tempting to think that the ferox followed these shoals, rather as we might expect pike to trail bream. Nowadays, however, I feel this is not the case.

New Methods for Ferox

It is not always necessary to fish for ferox at great depth, as the Victorians and Edwardians and even today's experts would have it, and the fish-finder tends to back up this speculation. I have heard about many ferox being caught close to the surface in the first few years of my obsession, and invariably discounted these as flukes. It wasn't until about 1991 that I began to change my mind and see things rather differently.

In 1990 and 1991 we located a head of ferox pretty well resident around some salmon parr cages. The food chain was obvious: the salmon parr were fed on a continual basis, and a great many pellets escaped to the water beneath the cages, where char concentrated as a result. And around the char concentration built up the ferox populations. True, there were not a great many ferox caught, but at least sport was almost reliable, and that certainly says something when it comes to ferox fishing. I continued to troll deep, as close to the cages as I could, and picked up fish in some encouraging numbers. However, I began to notice on the fish-finder screen that ferox were frequently just 10 or 20ft (3 or 6m) from the surface: this was interesting.

Then one (unsuccessful) day, I decided to try livebait: the fish farmer actually gave me a few small salmon from the nets, and I set them up as if I were fishing for pike. I fished both of them on a sliding float at around 30 to 40ft (9 to 12m) and nothing happened. Then I decided to fish one of the little baits a mere 15ft (4½m) down, and *very* shortly afterwards the first float sank and a big ferox – just over 10lb – was boated. Thereafter things changed fast.

Having spent the last three years ferox fishing, it seems to me that a feeding ferox frequently comes close to the surface in search of prey.

Notice I said a *feeding* ferox: I think it quite likely that a ferox that has already fed and which is digesting its prey *does* lie deep, perhaps even at 80ft (24m) or more. However, once the pangs of hunger begin to re-emerge, then in all likelihood the ferox begins to move up through the water looking for fish nearer the surface.

Suddenly all those 'fluke' captures began to make sense. This also coincided with a spate of fish being caught on small spinners on Loch Quoich, fished quickly behind the boat only 5 or 6ft (1½ to 1¾m) down. Clearly, the fact (dare I call it such) that feeding ferox move into the surface layers opens up vast new possibilities of fishing for them. Obviously, livebaiting is highly successful and I have enjoyed some nerve-tingling days when fishing this method. Whether you approve or not – and I myself can see a lot in it that worries me – for sheer suspense and excitement there is little to beat it.

Livebaiting for Ferox

Every book on pike fishing will explain the set-up. I use a slider float set by a stop-knot at anything between 10 and 20ft (3 and 6m). The bait is kept down to the required depth by a drilled bullet on the line, and a trace is made up with two size 8 or 10 trebles. The ideal bait will probably be a trout or salmon from a fish-farm cage around 3in (7½cm) long. Bigger than this and they are hard to manage under the float, and even harder for a ferox of 7 or 8lb to engulf the bait successfully.

Ideally the day will be relatively calm and I will manoeuvre round fish cages for any known ferox holding-point, letting the baits troll behind the boat after me. I will move very slowly, probably with no engine at all, just letting the wind push me here and there. I might occasionally scull a little bit with the oars to maintain direction, or even switch on the electric motor which will purr me around the water.

Action can be intense, and I have known as many as ten or fifteen strikes in a day with five ferox landed. You are bound to miss quite a few fish with this method because, as I have said, ferox are not natural predators in the way of pike. I find that it pays to delay the strike ten to fifteen

*A good trout – a young
ferox probably – taken from
the vicinity of the fish
cages. It is amazing what a
magnet these prove
(above).*

*A colossal fish, beautifully
shaped, taken by John
MacDonald on the troll.*

seconds, praying all the time that the big trout will not feel the resistance of the float and reject the bait. There is not much more to the method than that, but it opens up ferox fishing in a way never really discussed or realized before.

I appreciate that livebaiting might be more unacceptable to some people even than trolling – though I personally cannot see why. To my mind, the end justifies the means – and there is no finer end in game angling than the ferox trout! However, this tendency of big ferox to feed near the surface does make them vulnerable to the fly fisherman, and his method represents the ultimate challenge, to my mind. There are certain times and certain weathers when fly fishing for ferox becomes a possibility; I have tried it on many occasions, and just once or twice with some success.

Fly Fishing for Ferox
The weather appears to be critical if ferox are to come into the surface layers where they can be tackled on the fly. I have already mentioned that I prefer days with little wind, and those that are bright and warm seem to be excellent – going against everything that you would expect. In fact,

the water temperature has to rise above 50°F (10°C) before you can expect to find ferox in the upper layers. More conventionally, early morning seems to offer the best chance of success, and the ferox feeding spells that take place during this time can be quite intense affairs, even frightening sometimes. On many occasions now I have seen whole shoals of char that have been browsing near the top being pursued: it is not unusual to see five or six ferox furrowing through the water, hitting into the prey fish that escape in volcanic eruptions.

These are the times that the fly rod really can come into its own, and I have always gone for large lures fished on slow-sinking lines and pulled and retrieved quickly through the likely areas. I don't honestly think the type of lure makes that much difference; it is the size and the disturbance that it makes through the water that are the important things. Ferox are hunting hard in this type of mood, and providing the thing looks edible and is catchable it is very likely to be taken.

So far I would say that probably your best chance of catching ferox is to fish a livebait over a known holding area or to troll with artificials or naturals. However, once you feel at home on a

A massive Irish ferox, 17lb 12oz, taken by Des Elliott.

water and the weather is offering the right type of opportunities, there are real chances open on the fly. Moreover there is another occasion when the fly can produce the goods: each autumn some time in September, ferox begin to leave the deep waters of the loch, and at this time they become truly accessible. The last two weeks of September and the first week of October – right until the season ends – often offer the best chance of a ferox, certainly caught on a fly.

Once they are in the rivers, the ferox are very aggressive indeed, determined to defend their patch and chase off any intruder; this makes a large fly often seem irresistible. The second factor working in the angler's favour is that currents of the river tend to disguise the artificiality of a lure and impart extra life into it. Remember the ferox is now out of its usual bounds, so it is to some

extent vulnerable and certainly far more easily located. Obviously it is hard to know, without experience or guidance, exactly which streams will hold the ferox. It is wise to pay great attention to what the locals tell you, for most of them at some time in their lives have seen big fish in particular streams at this time of the year.

GREAT DAYS WITH FEROX

After years of effort I finally made contact with a ferox in 1988. It was an exciting encounter, and I wrote it all down soon afterwards; here is my account:

A wild night of wind and rain continued into morning. The waves had built up along the loch

The author with a ferox that did not get away.

until I was forced to flee to the sanctuary of the dam; it was very rough there, but fishable and I was glad still to be afloat.

I could do little but patrol the area, and found at once a shoal of char in the band between 40 to 70ft [12 to 20m], lying just off the pumping station. Around and around the shoal I patrolled, with the weather, if anything, worsening all the while. It was blowing more than half a gale now, but my mind was firmly on the job of working the baits and keeping the float roughly on its course. At around eleven o'clock, one rod tip bounced hard. I estimated my bait was perhaps 40ft [12m] down over recorded 50 to 55ft [15 to 16m] of water. It could not have been the bottom that hit my char! It was most probably a sunken tree or bush – or a fish. I reeled in. The char seemed untouched. I wish that dead fish could speak! I let it go down again and continued the troll.

The second and third times I crossed the place there was another tap; twenty minutes later, a fourth, and I was broadside to the waves off the pumping station: at the same place, the rod dipped and stayed down. I stopped the boat and moved back to the obstruction. I gave line: nothing happened. I held the boat steady: after a minute, just as I was sure I'd caught the bottom, line hissed of into the greyness beneath. The spool span, and I knew at last the char was taken.

The reel stopped; the line lay on the water, and I held the boat as best I could against the swell. Watching, praying, and then again something beneath began to move with solemn purpose. I clicked on the spool and wound down to the disappearing line. Everything grew tight and I hit the fish with all the might of the rod in my hands.

For that second I believed it was a boulder bottom again. But when the line zipped through the waves at the stern of the boat and off into the waste waters I knew that a ferox had struck like lightning. Very soon affairs were desperate. I'd never felt a fish of this power, nor experienced such a fight before; imagine a carp and a gigantic barbel fused together and you are close. The runs were breathtaking, even though the fish was deep, forcing me to follow into the swell. Soon I was motoring after it, trying to keep the line tight, trying to steer the boat and keep a proper speed behind it. I had not been able to reel in the other two outfits, and one caught in the propeller. At times the engine began to falter, and I knew that

if it should die there was no way I could play the fish and work the oars in waters such as these.

Heaven knows how many times the line had dropped slack and all contact had been lost: then it would grip tight and my heart would begin its beat again. Yet I was over the fish now: rain was teeming down, and there was almost as much water in the boat as outside it. The engine stuttered, and I sweated and swore; my back ached, but I was nearly there. I began to sense it: no fish could last long against a 3lb test curve carbon rod, 15lb line and direct vertical pressure. I glanced at the screen of the echo-sounder: I was over 114ft (35m); and then something else caught my eye, a

Predator expert Barry Rickards with a fantastic specimen of ferox from Loch Lomond.

A superb ferox taken with the snow still on the hill.

dot of red and black at 55ft (17m). There, in my vision, was my ferox. I stared, sure he would be mine now.

I kneeled on the bench and pumped, but still he would dive and line would be lost. I saw him at 60ft (18m) and again at 70ft (20m); then I watched the missile plummet to the bottom of the screen. At 12.31pm the rod suddenly felt slack in my hands, and a fast-moving speck disappeared from my vision.

In despair, I worked the limping boat back to the base, my eyes closed by the rain. My dull brain sought a solution. Not enough line given on the second run? The gyrations of the boat? The constant changes of pressure on the hook-point that had worn itself free? Then elation filled me. There are not many men to have battled twenty minutes with a giant brown trout. I must at last be doing things half right! I had come so close, and knew I would not turn back now.

Well, even after the dismay of losing that particular fish I did not turn back, but continued with my quest for ferox; and other, thrilling days were to follow.

There was, for example, the first fish that we were to catch on a livebait, the day I shared a boat with that excellent angler and friend Chris Bennett. The morning had been unproductive, even though we were trolling around the trout cages on Loch Arkaig, generally quite a productive area. We stopped for lunch at about one o'clock and I decided that this was the day, if any, to put my livebaiting theories into practice; I therefore travelled down to the trout farm that was in existence in those days and brought back half-a-dozen little fish.

Chris and I both set up what in effect was simple pike tackle, with a sliding float each set to work the bait at around 20ft (6m) or so. We let the boat amble around in the mild breeze, watching the floats bob and dip here and there, sending out ripples on the quite calm surface.

Suddenly, when it was quite close to the boat, Chris's float simply disappeared; I remember it going down with such a force that there was an audible plop as it went. We looked at each other. We hardly knew what to do in such a case, and were torn between giving the fish time, and fearing it would feel the resistance of the float. In the end we decided to compromise, and after five or six seconds Chris picked up the rod and struck hard.

The fish beneath tugged back nearly as hard! The look on Chris's face was quite one to behold as the rod hooped over – the tip, I remember, was actually pulled under the surface. The fight was not particularly dramatic, more one of give-and-take as the fish gradually came up towards the surface. Then we saw the float, and knew that the trout, or whatever it was, couldn't be more than 4 or 5ft (1¼ to 1½m) beneath us; we strained to look for its shape.

We needn't have bothered, because suddenly, right before our eyes, a yard from the boat and a yard out of the water, hung a massive ferox. We just gasped – and the fish crashed back into the loch to dive back down at least another 15ft (4½m). It was pure elation that night: not everybody catches a ferox of nearly 13lb on their first serious day's outing, and I realized that a technique had been found that would stay. And stay it most certainly did.

The following year saw me on Arkaig again, fishing very hard with the livebaiting method. Of many happy days, one springs particularly to mind: again, it was very still, only this time quite bright. I began fishing at about nine o'clock in the morning with my frequent companion, Roger Miller, and within ten minutes we had registered our first but dropped run. By midday we had made contact with five ferox, but each time either the bite had been missed or the fish had come off after a few agonizing seconds. It was devastating, and we were nearly at our wits' end.

A close-up of a ferox, with the book above it to help with identification.

A super Mask fish.

Shortly afterwards Roger had to leave; scarcely had his car disappeared from view when the float once again sank. The ferox weighed 6lb – not a great fish, but a beautiful, compact powerful trout, and I was elated. An hour later another float went, and this time the ferox was just under 9lb; things were most definitely looking up.

It was a quarter to six and I had three livebaits working around the boat: the float furthest away from me suddenly began to bob and weave violently for some ten or fifteen seconds, then everything went quiet again. Then the mid-way float began to show obvious signs of movement, running this way, a yard that way, almost slanting under; before it, too, went quiet again.

By now I was quite alert and tense, waiting for something to happen – and it did: the float nearest to me simply disappeared. It was 10½lb of fabulous ferox. Poor Roger! I remember being hardly able to tell him that night in the bar when he bounded down expectantly to hear my news; he took it like a true ferox man.

These were not fly-caught fish, but when talking trout like these, who really cares? The lochs can be so difficult, and ferox so few, that you have got to fish for them in the most sensible and practical way you can think of. Mind you, a ferox on a fly is quite something and I've seen it happen more than once… and so has Rab, and I don't think he'll ever forget the occasion! It was right at the end of the trout season and the rain had been torrential, flooding the river so that it swept into the loch more like the great brown Ganges than a mountain stream.

Still, all that water must have stirred up the fish, and it had drawn at least one ferox to the estuary mouth. And that was where Rab took his, one rain-soaked day on a fly meant for a late-running salmon. In fact for several minutes, Rab thought he had a salmon on, a big salmon, he said. And then the fish broke surface: a big, beautiful trout with colours as vivid as the Highland setting all around. It lay on a bed of autumn leaves and the rain soaked it, and we all gathered round just marvelling at its extraordinary beauty.

12 FISHING FOR CHAR

My long and serious interest in ferox led inevitably to an equal passion for char, a species that originally attracted me as a mere preyfish but which rapidly became something far more special to me. The char is a lovely fish, the star of those glorious, deep glacial lochs scattered through the mountain ranges of Scotland, the Lake District and parts of Ireland.

CHAR: THE SPECIES

Our char are something of an aberration, and certainly the original fish was probably sea-going, merely returning to fresh water from time to time to spawn – just like those populations that now thrive in Labrador and Greenland, for example. In Britain too, you don't always find char down deep, as old legend would have it; in fact, the char has a complex and a fascinating lifestyle, possibly beyond all others in Britain.

Identifying Features

The Victorians recognized many different sub-species of char, even going so far as to give them distinct names. In my growing experience I have come to the conclusion that there is hardly any such thing as a typical char, for I have certainly witnessed an enormous variation in coloration and spotting patterns, not to mention size. Indeed, I remember one particular day in the mid-eighties, when I was first learning how to catch these fish, I caught eleven in a single afternoon – something of a triumph for me then. I soon realized that every single fish was just a little bit different from its predecessor, perhaps a hint of green here or a dash of blue there, or unusually bold markings on the pectorals. And

Char loch in the depths of winter when the shoals are down deep.

this was from a single water where you would have expected all the char to have looked as alike as sardines in a tin. Char simply confound you from first to last.

Char of Record Size

And char have confounded everybody over the last six years or so when it comes to their size. For many years the record char in this country hovered around 2lb, and a very good fish indeed was half that weight. Of course, this was always very different from the sea-going variety, where 4 to 6lb fish were common and many went on to double that weight. It now seems that in certain areas freshwater char are following this trend.

Since the late 1980s the char record in Scotland has gone mad. The first major fish to attract my attention was the 4lb 13oz monster taken, I think in 1987. Next I heard of a 5lb 7oz fish that was being considered by the record committee, and then Joy Hurst and I actually landed a 5lb 10oz specimen; however, we didn't even bother to claim as we heard about a larger fish within a week. That weighed 6lb 1oz, but it was quickly superseded by a fish of 6lb 9oz, then one of 7lb 2oz, next a 7lb 7oz fish, then an eight-pounder and now, I believe, a fish of well over 9lb. By the time this book finally makes print, I have no doubt that a 10lb char will have been landed somewhere in Scotland.

Quite why these super char have begun to emerge is not absolutely clear: most people tend to agree that it is something to do with the fish farms that have appeared on several loch systems. The feeling is that pellets drift through the net where they are taken by gathering char shoals, and it is this high protein diet which makes char grow bigger and faster and explains the boom in size. Perhaps there is more to it than that; many fish farms have mass escapes of small smolts and parr, thus releasing a great number of prey-sized fish into otherwise relatively barren food chains. Possibly larger char capitalize on this, become fish-eaters and rocket forwards in size. From this it would seem that our freshwater char have always been held back, limited by the poorness of their environment, and that it needs only a slight tilt in foodstocks or fertility for certain fish to benefit and attain the sort of size generally seen only around the Greenland coast. Whatever the reason, the result is quite plain: char now offer more than a merely quaint challenge. These are big and beautiful fish, and interest every game angler who comes into contact with them.

Char Habits and Lifestyle

I soon began to realize that the char year in most Scottish lochs is fascinating just in itself, and

many hours afloat with a fish locater soon taught me a great deal regarding the char's habits. Certainly it appeared that during the winter and well into the spring the char would shoal up into vast congregations and hang quite deep, though exactly when was dependent on the weather and water temperatures. Then, it was not uncommon to find them in groups of anything up to 200 or 300yd (180 to 275m) long and 100yd (90m) or more across, and what's more, the band of fish would often be 20 or 30ft (6 to 9m) deep! In fact, from what I could tell, it was not at all unusual for all the char in even a very large loch to group together like this in two or three vast shoals. Quite why this happens I would not presume to say, but my research does indicate that this is a fact.

Generally, when a shoal like this is located it seems to lie at anything between 60 and 100ft (18 to 30m) deep. There may be certain variations to this, and sometimes fish will come to the 30ft (9m) or even the 20ft (6m) contour, and at the other extreme I have often seen them way below 100ft (30m). In fact, according to scientists at Loch Ness, certain species of char have been turned up beneath the 800ft (240m) mark! Certainly the char is a more-than-adaptable fish.

From some time in May, once the water begins to rise over 50°F (10°C), the char begin to change their habits. As the summer really gets under way, many fish will come to the surface, especially at dusk, during the night and at dawn. The huge shoals of the winter and spring seem to break up, and at this time smaller groups of fish, often only twenty or forty strong, seem to dot themselves around the water in small shoals of great confusion. On a still, warm summer's night you might row home and see sprinklings of char dimpling the surface here, there and virtually everywhere. Moreover, a lot of fish will also move into any shallow, weedy parts of the loch and spend most of the summer in water that is frequently less than 20ft (6m) deep. So the old concept of the char hugging the coldest water as summer wears on seems to be blown out of existence – or at least, a good number of char have learnt to adapt, and have got to know that comparatively prolific food sources are open for them around the margins and in the bays. Often, happily, it is the largest char that move into the shallow water, thereby making themselves much more vulnerable to anglers.

In early September things begin to change again. Certainly, by the second week, char from all over the loch are beginning to move towards incoming rivers and streams to search out their spawning sites. Of course, there is a well documented second spawning of different fish that takes place in some waters in February, but as far as fisherman are concerned, it is the autumn spawners that really attract attention. From mid-September to early October, therefore, large numbers of often large char are grouped into quite accessible areas, and at times the fishing can be sensational.

CHAR: THE QUARRY

Let's now look at fishing possibilities for char. Nobody would want to be out on those lochs in the winter, and anyway the season does not begin until spring begins to creep through the glens. It is possible to catch char at this early date and I have done it, but I would not really recommend it as a constant habit. I have found that once a shoal of char shows up on the screen it is possible to jig small flies amongst the shoal and get occasional takes. You would think the fishing would be frantic for, after all, hundreds of thousands of char must be looking at the flies as they dance past; and yet takes are few and far between. If I remember, my best day employing this method was a mere nine fish! Very often they

The char and the fly.

A huge fish – a very short-lived record – taken down deep in the late spring.

will not feed at all. Quite why this is so is hard to know: it could be that they are feeding either on microscopic food items or not feeding at all.

If you are determined to catch your char it is, as I have said, quite a simple matter to let line out to the required depth and jig small flies – I have found red ants to be as good as anything – through the shoal. A light rod, a fixed-spool reel and 3 or 4lb line seem to work well for this method; the flies can be taken down by a ½oz (14g) drilled bullet on the line. It is an easy task to tie a piece of cotton wool or something similar to mark off the correct depth. Ideally the day will be relatively calm (although this rarely happens in the spring-time on large lochs) or otherwise the boat will move too fast for effective jigging. Of course, this method is hardly full of grace or skill, but often the fish make up for everything you might suffer.

The real excitement of char fishing begins around June when, as I have said, the fish are on the surface and especially moving into shallow water on a near-permanent basis. In my experience those that come to the surface in the late evening are almost impossible to catch. They seem uniquely sensitive to the approach of the boat and the splash of the oars, and I find it extremely difficult to get within sensible casting range. At times I have simply drifted and waited for fish to come to me, but even then success is far from assured. I have, it is true, picked up one or two fish using the tiniest imaginable buzzers and black dry flies, generally tied on a No 18, a No 20 or a No 22. Bigger flies have seemed to be a total waste of time.

It is when the better fish move into the shallow weedy bays that the real drama begins. They still tend to move in small groups which make a certain amount of disturbance, and can, therefore, be stalked along the bank, on islands or stealthily in boats. Nearly all imitative flies will stand a chance, especially beetles, corixae and so on. The char, which can be very large ones, are obviously well on the feed and really routing in these fertile parts of the loch. Takes are very positive, and my word, don't they fight! Note your tackle: it really makes no sense at all to go into the weedy, snaggy areas with leaders much less than 5 or 6lb bs.

Char in these shallows can be picked up at any time during the day, although early morning and evening often prove to be the best. But not always: there have been times when I have experienced the best sport over mid-day and in the early afternoon. You really just cannot tell for sure, so it pays to be out there as long as possible with as much concentration as you can muster.

I ought to say that the deeper water immediately adjacent to the shallows is often very productive, often for the very biggest char of all. I suppose it is possible to fish these deep areas (around 20 to 40ft/6 to 12m) with fly, but I have to admit that the big char that I have caught have tended to come when I was trolling lures, ferox-style. As I have said before, this might not appeal to everybody, and I can understand why, but then again, if it is really big char that you are after, it is a method worth thinking about. Sometimes it pays to rest a shallow bay for a while anyway, and a few trolls of half a mile or so with a good, lively plug will provide a bit of distraction and often a very welcome, large fish. The choice, obviously, is yours.

For sheer excitement as far as I am concerned, the peak of char fishing is reached in mid- and late September. The glens are at their very best then too, resplendent in burnished bracken, and often the stags are beginning to roar at night. You are immediately aware of the vital current of life running through the Highlands at this time, a current that is certainly vibrating through the char that are flocking to the river mouths preparatory to spawning. Now it is possible to fish for them in quick, dashing water with large reservoir-type lures, fished quickly down and across. The bow waves that often chase the fly, and the wrist-wrenching tugs that follow are quite amazing. To my mind, the fly pattern is not critical at all, and I have had success with all manner of shapes and colours: if anything, size is the key and I would not go much smaller than anything tied on a size 6.

There are not always char in the rivers during this period, and you tend to find that groups of twenty to forty fish will come and go. Most often they come some time during the night; dawn is generally one of the hottest periods. Indeed, when the weather is still and calm, it is possible to see shoals crashing in the surface film, showering after minnows or sticklebacks. I cannot think of a more glorious place to fish for more glorious quarry than the char in such circumstances. Generally – although of course there are exceptions – the char begin to melt away as the morning wears on, but occasional fish will come in and be caught. Late afternoon sees the char begin to appear in numbers, and certainly those last few casts before dinner can often be wildly successful.

The Threat to Char Numbers

From what I have said, it might appear that the char scene is exceptionally buoyant, especially in Scotland. Certainly, there are still large stocks of average fish, and the size of some individuals probably continues to escalate. However, I think we would be wise to realize that there are limited numbers of these very big fish, and we should respect every one that we catch. Char are quite vulnerable, especially when they migrate, and the news of many prime locations has spread throughout Scotland and well into England. It is therefore hardly surprising that char would be put under a certain amount of pressure at these key times; it was quite common a few years ago to see people leave the river with huge bags of fish over their shoulder. I, and many others, believed that this was a great mistake: it is quite likely that even a large loch only supports a relatively small number of big fish, and culling them like this on the spawning grounds is bound to be counter-productive, and the effects felt quite quickly. Thankfully, nowadays it is much more usual to see anglers return char upon capture, or even to give up altogether after a fish or two has been taken.

There are other threats as well: very recently there were plans afoot to begin commercial char netting on may of the large lochs. I am very unsure about the possibilities that this move would have: certainly my contacts in Germany and Austria where this happens are very hostile indeed, and say that commercial netting has affected their stocks in the direct way. Certain parts of the Highlands could possibly do with more employment, but not by risking one of the country's most precious resources. Char stocks are noble and historical, and we must be very careful how we treat them.

They are under other threats from man besides netting. The decline of char stocks in England and the Lake District has been well charted, and that seems to be as a result of urban developments on the banks of these large lakes. Char and modern development do not go together, that is plain, so let us hope for all our sakes that at least the stocks of Scotland are left intact and free.

CHAR DAYS

When char forsake the depths to feed in zones of the water where the fly fisherman can easily make inroads, some marvellous fishing can result. One occasion I particularly remember was a pleasant day in high summer when I was fishing Loch Quoich, the far end, miles from any road and really only approachable by boat; the walk along the shoreline is gruelling, so I chose the boat! My primary purpose that day was ferox, but when I moored at the bottom end of the loch for lunch I

became aware of fish rising quite busily in all the bays, just out from the margins in around 2 to 4ft (½ to 1¼m) of water. I expected these fish to be brown trout and decided to try to take a few back home with me.

The fish were not trout at all, but char. They were very easy to catch that day and fell to straightforward trout tactics – small wet flies pulled back quite quickly just under the surface. Most interesting – biologically, anyway – was the fact that every one of these char was slightly different, perhaps coloration, or spotting or shape, just something that made it quite different from its immediate fellow.

Some seven or eight miles beneath Quoich stretch the waters of Inchlaggan, a comparatively small loch at the head of Loch Garry. Inchlaggan was formed when Garry itself was dammed and the water level rose many feet, flooding the meadows alongside what was a river. The river course is still very easily traced as it runs through Inchlaggan today, and the char almost certainly follow this much deeper water when they move out of Garry to investigate the smaller water. However, very often, and in the summer especially, char will flood out of the channel and

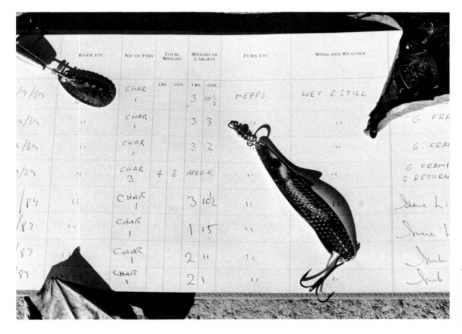

A remarkable page from a hotel fishing book. Just look at the size and number of these char, all taken on the same day.

begin to feed voraciously on the shallows either side. When this happens big fish – far bigger than the Quoich specimens – can be taken on the fly.

On this next occasion I was gillying for a fisherman from the south. He was keen to catch anything, and I had a feeling that char might be the most obliging quarry. Accordingly we rode out of Garry, under the bridge and into Inchlaggan. There was nothing much showing until we approached the top of that particular piece of water, about a quarter of a mile (½km) from where the River Garry enters. On the extensive flats there, so shallow that the weed was showing everywhere, a great many fish were rising, and so prolific were the rises that I knew at once we were not looking at feeding trout. I managed to manoeuvre the boat very quietly close to the biggest congregation of fish, and soon my friend was hooking a char with nearly every cast, on quite large, standard wet flies. Most of the fish taken that day were between 1lb and 2lb but for the wildest excitement, a fish of nearly 4lb was boated just before tea.

Following such success we often visited the area again over the next week, and found the shoals of char operating in much the same way over much the same area; and they always obliged and fell to fly-fishing tactics. Since that day I have come to realize that for a good part of the summer at least, char, both big and small, like to use the shallows just as much as the brown trout, if not even more so.

Char are not confined to Inchlaggan by any means, and inhabit dozens of lochs throughout Scotland. Arkaig is one of the most prolific waters, and in fact, my wife and I were lucky enough to hold the char record for a few days on that very water. It was early in the season in 1990, and I arrived in the north to hear rumours of a 5lb-plus char that had fallen to the lures of a very famous ferox angler, John McDonald. Our day of excitement took place in May as we trawled along the deep south shore of the slightly choppy Arkaig. Midday approached and my wife, Joy had the rods when a fish took the 5in (13cm) flat fish plug, travelling at 25 to 30ft (8 to 9m) down. She played the fish for a while, then handed me the rod for an opinion. I agreed with her that it felt like a good-sized trout, and was about to hand back the rod when 10 or 15ft (3 or 4m) below the boat I saw a flash or white-edged pectorals, which could only mean char. I also saw the great and shadowy size of the fish.

'Joy,' I said, far more calmly than I actually felt, 'we've broken the char record!' So for a while it proved. I admit I wrested the rod from her when I saw the size of the fish, and played it out for the last minute or so. There's chauvinism for you, but the fish was safely boated, and from 4lb 13oz the record moved to our own 5lb 9oz monster. I had always wondered what it would be like to hold a record and be named in the eternal halls of fame, and for ten days it seemed that this dream would become a reality. Then rumours circulated the glens of a 6lb 1oz fish, rumours which soon proved to be correct. Fame and fortune are fickle jades, for almost as quickly the record moved on to John McDonald himself once more, this time with a 7lb fish. And it didn't stop there, but now hovers just below the 10lb mark, making our own monster look quite a middling fish indeed.

So far I've been talking about large, deep waters, true Ice Age waters, places where the char have a wide variety of habitats and have probably lived for many thousands of years. Originally I believed these to be the only places to hold char, but I was quite mistaken: in the summer of 1992 I was taken to a very small lochan indeed, about 15 miles (24km) from Fort William, a water which overturned my assumptions. It was quite a climb to reach it, a very small place of perhaps 10 to 15 acres (4–6ha), situated on a moor. The amazing thing was that this particular water was shallow, no more than 7 or 8ft (2 to 2½m) deep and yet it held char in abundance. In just a short period we managed to land three fish, all quite healthy, though small at about 6 or 7oz (170 to 200g).

I only mention this last lochan to emphasize how much there is that we still don't yet know about char; that they are a species continually capable of springing surprises, fish that offer countless opportunities to the fly angler if only he really knew it.

13 A VIEW OF IRELAND

The great fish of Ireland have always been salmon and trout, bream and pike. The bream, however, has been generally spurned, used as pig food or fertilizer at best; and the pike has always been a villain, in an heroic sort of way, to the Irish. They have been able to accept that it is big and ferocious, but never to forgive the way it preys on salmon and trout stocks. Game fish are the real gems of Ireland, and few Irish anglers would ever consider anything capable of beating, in particular, the wild Irish trout.

Ireland is a country fabulously rich in trout waters, boasting magnificent limestone lakes set in moist, warm landscape. Moreover, wind and cloud are fairly constant, the two elements that make the fly fisher's dream complete. I suppose Ireland is most famous for its great Western loughs, Corrib, Conn and Mask in particular, but there are many others that merit attention. Here, Richard Johnston gives a personal introduction to a slightly lesser known Irish water that merits attention. Richie is a young but most accomplished angler; recently he has been selected to fish in the Irish Fly Fishing team against Scotland.

FISHING IRELAND'S LAKES

For a small island, Ireland offers a huge choice of fishing to the angler. There are thousands of miles of rivers of all sizes, and thousands of lakes as well. As well as its coarse fishing, which at times can be breathtaking, Ireland offers possibly the finest trout fishing in Europe. Wild brown trout are present in most waters, and the angler's greatest problem is choosing where to fish.

Over the years, many Irish lakes have become famous worldwide for their fishing, places such as Lough Mask in County Mayo, known for its hard-fighting trout which move so freely to the fly, and its ferox trout which grow to over 20lb in weight. Scores of anglers come here every year and troll for these huge legendary trout, and the magnificent scenery just adds to the enjoyment of fishing this beautiful lake.

Then there is Lough Corrib, which is second to none as far as early season fishing is concerned. Sheeling, in the midlands, is very popular with

A magnificent Irish trout.

English anglers, and every season they take great trout when fishing the mayfly, sedges and buzzers. But as far as I am concerned, the jewel in the crown is the heart of Ireland, Lough Ennell. Ennell is situated near Mullingar in County Westmeath; it is an average-sized lake by Irish standards, about five miles (8km) long and nearly two miles (3km) wide, and has really seen the highs and lows of Irish trout fishing.

History of Lake Ennell

Until the 1970s, Ennell was regarded as one of the finest fisheries in the country. Its crystal-clear water and limestone bottom produced trout of the highest quality, and its feeder streams were perfect for spawning, with plenty of gravel and stones. Originally the lake was known as Lake Belvedere. On the eastern shore of the lake is a huge country house set in a lovely forested area: Belvedere House, and there are not many better sights than when drifting past it, fishing amongst the shallows at Goose and Goslin Island.

In the years it was known as Belvedere Lake the fishing was spectacular. Trolling and fly fishing were practised the most: either you could drift along, casting amongst the many rocks and islands searching out a cruising trout; or you could sit and wait with a dry fly. The lake's fly life was very rich, with great hatches of mayflies, sedges and lake olives. Dapping was also a favourite with local anglers. One hundred years ago, in 1884, the lake produced a trout to a local angler which has never been equalled in Ireland by rod and line. The lucky man was William Mears, who was trolling the lake in the hope of a big pike. But his spoon was seized by a large trout of massive proportions: it weighed a staggering 26lb 2oz, and can be seen today in the museum in Dublin. The size of this fish was a credit to the lake's feeding and fish-growing potential.

The lake continued to fish well until the 1970s, but then as usual, Man had to come along and ruin it. In the mid- to late seventies anglers seemed to notice that their catches were deteriorating rapidly, and that the water quality was not of its usual clarity; before this it had been possible to see 15 to 20ft (4½ to 6m) below the surface with ease. Fly hatches became minimal. Many questions were asked to find out the answers to the problems – and were found out quite quickly: it transpired that the local council was using

Irish trout fishing in a frame.

Lough Ennell as a dump for its raw, untreated sewage. As a result of this, the number of anglers visiting the lake became virtually nil; local guesthouses, gillies and boat-hire people were all affected, as well as the trout.

To the anglers, the council's behaviour was like a red rag to a bull. For nearly a decade they fought the battle with the local councils and government officials to clean up the lake; the fisheries board tried hard, but to little effect. If you were on the lake during this period you would see huge mounds of sewage floating in the water, all with a rotten smell coming from them. Only the die-hard locals fished the lake then, but with little success.

In the early eighties there was a change for the better. The voices of both local anglers and the fisheries board were eventually listened to, and slowly the sewage problem was sorted out by means of a treatment plant. But still the lake was not in good condition and so the local angling club stepped in; they could have just sat back and hoped that Mother Nature would repair the lake, but she does need some help sometimes. The rivers where the trout used to run up and spawn were full of sewage; they had also been straightened by the famous 'dredgers'. The Lough Ennell Trout Preservation Association raised money in any way they could, and bought as much gravel as they could get. Every weekend and spare moment they had, they were on the nursery streams with the fishery board: new runs were made, and gravel was put all over the river bed. Slowly but surely the numbers of trout running up to spawn increased. At one stage it was only a few hundred fish; the fisheries also released unfed fry into the streams; and fly hatches returned as the lake's bottom became cleaner.

By 1994 Ennell had become probably Ireland's best fishery. Now, the feeder streams are teeming with small trout, as are the shallows of the lake, too, and the water is very clear. The average weight of the trout is returning to its norm at about 1lb 12oz; during the problem era the aver-

age size was between 3 and 4lb. This sounds good from an angler's point of view, but lakes need a good balance of fish, small and large. Fly hatches during 1994 were huge, particularly the mayfly; at times it was so prolific that the lake was like a green carpet, and you couldn't fill your kettle without getting mayflies in it. For the visitor this would be a most exciting time to visit the lake.

Tackle and Techniques on the Loughs
From about 10 May, mayflies start to appear on the lake, though the exact date depends on the weather, which needs to be fairly warm. At first the trout seem to find this natural phenomenon a bit odd, but after a few days, as hatches get better, they start to feed on flies with more confidence. Standard wet fly fishing from a drifting boat is most popular, using three flies on a floating line; most Irish anglers use 10ft to 11ft fly rods for this. Successful flies are Yellow and Green Fanwings, Grey Whulfs, Golden Olive Bumbles,

A superb Corrib trout taken on the spoon.

The magnificent Western lakes with their huge castles.

Goslings, Green Peters and a favourite of mine is a Raymond.

The lake is generally quite shallow, mostly from 6 to 11ft (1¾ to 3¼m) deep. As the flies blow out onto the lake after being in the bushes, the fish feed heavily on them in the shallows. Some flies get blown into the deeper water, and the fish can be taken here as well. On the calmer days, in the lea of an island, some terrific dry fly fishing can be had; the local anglers catch a great many fish using this method, including some very big ones. This year some anglers came in off the lake after a few hours with three or four trout weighing a total of 15 to 16lb; a few larger fish up to 10lb were also taken.

Nowadays the lake has a very good head of fish in the 12oz to 1lb 8oz class. On most lakes these fish are of takeable size, but on Ennell this is not so: the official fisheries size limit is 12in (30cm) but the Lough Ennell Trout Preservation Association changed their limit to 14in (35cm); they think, and I agree, that there is no point in taking fish under 1lb 8oz when there is a good chance of a 3lb to 5lb fish. During the day is not only the best time to fish as, after about ten days of the mayfly, spent gnats appear on the lake in the evenings. These are mayflies which have come out to lay eggs on the water, and which die soon after this. Many do not get a chance to do so, as greedy trout feed heavily on them. A favourite pattern of these gnats is the Copydex body, quite deadly on Ennell.

Dapping is also very popular on Lough Ennell during the mayfly; most Irish anglers use telescopic dapping rods. One thing is very important with dapping on Irish loughs: plenty of backing on your reel. It was T.C. Kingsmill Moore who described Ennell trout as 'taking like a runaway train'. Huge trout fall to this method every season. Another important item is a good-sized landing net, as I found out this year, dropping a fish of about 6lb from a net which was simply too small for the job at hand.

Ennell is not just a mayfly lake, and after the excitement of mayflies there are great hatches of sedges; one local angler told me that he got even better fishing this year during the sedges. Other lakes in the area are worth a visit, such as Lough Owel and Lough Sheelin; Owel is a lively fishery all season, with both wild and stocked trout. It is famous for its hatch of Green Peters, a huge sedge; the trout love them.

Lough Sheelin is another favourite of mine, being about twelve miles (19km) from Mullingar. It, too, has had its pollution problems in the past, but hopefully the progress made in the last few years will continue. Sheelin generally has a huge hatch of mayfly, and this year was no exception, with many fine fish falling to spent gnats, wet and dry mayflies and, of course, the dap. August and September are good times to fish Ennell and Sheelin. Dapping brings up plenty of good fish, and it was on Lough Sheelin in August 1991 that I caught my largest brown trout on the dap.

Dapping on Lough Sheelin

That day was not particularly suitable for dapping, which I had intended to do, as it was very bright and there was only a light wind. Pat Cleere, a Dublin tackle dealer, and I fly fished for two to three hours, moving a few fish but connecting with none. After a good brew-up on the shore we were pleased to see the breeze increase, and numbers of daddy-longlegs were blown out onto the water. Suddenly the area we were fishing, between Sailor's Garden and Bog Bay, became alive with fish, rolling lazily at the daddies. Quickly we put out the dapping rods; soon I was into a lively fish of around 1lb 8oz, and Pat was stuck into an even better one, which took him around the back of the boat; after a good fight I netted a lovely golden fish for him of about 2lb 8oz, which he was very pleased with. I put up two fresh daddies and let the line out about 15yd (14m) from the boat. As we passed a weedy point, a huge bow wave came across the front of the boat; at first I thought it was coming towards Pat's dap, but it continued past it and made a great lunge at my dancing daddies.

I quickly lowered the rod, and then lifted into the fish of dreams. The fight was typical of a large Irish trout, hard, strong runs towards the lake bed, then circling the boat a few times. Fifteen minutes later, after a few heart-stopping jumps, Pat netted this beautiful monster: it weighed 9lb 13oz, a cracking fish on the dap. This story proves that anybody, even in the wrong conditions, can hit a leviathan on these waters, where hopefully the fishing for wild brown trout will be second to none for many years to come.

A shot that gives an idea of the scale of these huge Irish waters.

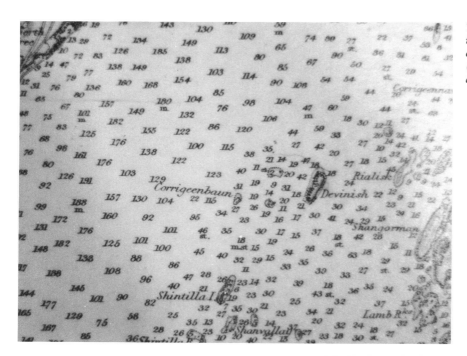

The depths are all-important when you are on waters two or three miles (3 to 5km) wide. The old charts can be invaluable.

DAPPING

Dapping is the concept of using the wind to billow out the line and allow a large natural or artificial fly to skitter on the surface in as natural a way as possible. In theory, nothing sounds simpler; in practice, things are just a little bit more difficult – but even so, dapping can be one of the most rewarding way of fishing any stillwater, large or small. The surprising thing is that dapping still tends to be seen as an Irish art form, even though it works just as well on English and even Scottish waters to those few anglers prepared to try it.

My own introduction to dapping came in Ireland on Loughs Mask and Corrib under the tuition of Des Elliott. In the west of Ireland Des is widely regarded as a big fish man, and his tally of enormous ferox trout is enviable; however, this hides the fact that he is just as happy with a fly rod. I shall leave it to Des to explain the tackle and technique needed for successful dapping:

> Because we are generally after trout or perhaps sea trout on some of the loughs, the tackle might sound a bit on the light side, but most fish hooked

Hunting mayfly.

are landed. A size 10 hook is the norm, but it must have a wide bend to take the two natural mayflies that you will want to put on it. You simply hook them through the thorax and they should stay on. Mayflies are so prolific around many Irish loughs at certain times of the year that you can pick them off the bushes on the shore before you start fishing; it's as easy as that providing they're out in numbers. If they're not, you could have problems, and that's why there is a thriving schoolboy industry on Lough Corrib – the kids collect them and then sell them to the anglers the next day. I'm not sure what the going rate is at the moment, but I should think it's somewhere between 50p and £1 for a dozen; you'll probably have to bargain a bit! Make sure the flies are in decent condition.

Telescopic fibreglass rods seem to be all the rage, generally extending to about 14ft in length. The good thing about the rods being telescopic is that if the wind becomes very strong and the full rod is difficult to manage, then you can dip down a section and fish with a rod of reduced length. This is a system that works very well indeed.

Centre pin reels are used uniformly, with plenty of nylon backing of about 15lb bs; to this is attached a length of synthetic floss anything between 10 and 12ft in length. That is attached to a leader which should be something between 4 and 8ft of nylon of about 6lb bs. These are rough measurements, because they tend to be changed according to the weather conditions; for example in a very stiff wind you probably won't need the floss, which is only there to help catch the breeze if there isn't much of it about. Equally you can use a slightly heavier leader, because hardly any, if any, is put on the water.

The trick is to let the fly sit on the water and drift ahead of you, in front of the boat. You can lift it off from time to time and let it settle again in a natural way; but that is the key – your mayfly has to behave as much like the real thing as you can make it.

Drifting on a water the size of Corrib can cover miles and you will be passing over many scores of fish as you go. However, this can be a frustrating way of fishing. For example, supposing you see a good fish move right or left of your drift – if you

Richie Johnston sets up in a perfect, sheltered bay.

Richie on the dap.

His father draws first blood.

are on your own, there is very little you can do except let your fly move directly in front of you. Ideally you need two men dapping and one man on the oars so that he can redirect the boat if you see a really good fish that you want to go after. The fish move upwind and you will see them rising, taking naturals in a lazy way. Yours is very likely to be accepted providing that it does not skitter along the surface or look unnatural in any way. At this time of the year there is no doubt that the dapped mayfly beats a wet fly hands down, and brings in whole baskets of fish – even grilse if they are running. Moreover it's a satisfying and fascinating way to fish, and you are imitating nature to the utmost degree.

Mayflies are not the only flies that can be used with the dapping method, and big sedges and craneflies (daddy-longlegs) are probably just as good, both sides of the Irish Sea. Also, there is no need to despair if naturals are not available, as artificials will work nearly as well. There is a good choice of artificial daddy-longlegs, in particular, on the market and most work well providing they are really big and bushy. There are two ways of working the artificial: you can either let the fly sit quietly on the surface while you simply maintain a tightish line, or you can make it work a little bit by lifting or

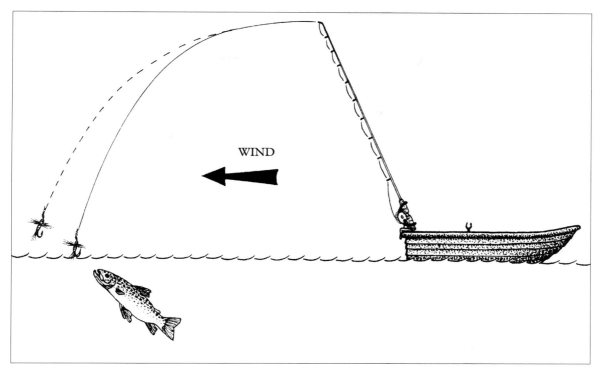

Fig. 31 *Dapping is one of the most deadly and the most enjoyable methods of catching fish. The great secret lies in the use of a floss line which floats on the wind, carrying it out, allowing the dry fly to skip around on the surface as much like a natural as it is possible to fish a fly. There is no problem with fly line or leader, and indeed, very short leaders of just one or two feet (30 to 60cm) are necessary to keep the fly firmly under control. Too long a leader and the fly will simply catch in the wind and blow here and there, rarely touching the water.*

shaking the rod tip. A good deal depends on the chop at the time; the heavier the wave probably the less you will need to work the fly. However, these are very rough guidelines indeed and generally it is just as well to experiment a little.

As I have said, there is no reason at all that dapping should be restricted to Ireland, or even to boat fishing alone. Come to think of it, my very first meeting with the method was not actually with Des at all, but over thirty years ago on that first water of mine, Tintwhistle. I noticed in the late summer that the trout were coming up to daddy-longlegs that were being blown in profusion off the bank; in fact, they were picking them up just a few yards from the bank. The next day, without knowing anything about dapping, I collected a few live ones and fished them on a small

bare hook; the winds were strong enough for me to drift them out and they would be taken at once. The bailiff was suspicious at my new and

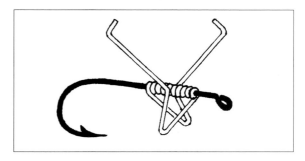

Fig. 32 *A purpose-built dapping hook: the spring folds over to encase a live insect, usually one or two mayflies themselves. Occasionally other insects, even bluebottles, will fit the bill.*

The wind can hardly be too strong for the dapping method...

... But things are more pleasant when it drops back to manageable proportions.

resounding success rate, and checked up on me, telling me firmly that artificial flies only could be used. It didn't matter: I actually found an artificial nearly as good and the excitement wasn't diminished in the least.

A lot of our stillwaters are small and intimate, and the fish undoubtedly feed a great deal on terrestrial flies, especially large ones blown in from the surrounding bankside vegetation. When all this is happening, dapping is surely the most efficient and certainly the most exciting way of presenting a fly.

THE CHARM OF THE WESTERN LAKES

Frederic Buller is the happy owner of a delightful whitewashed cottage in Ballinrobe, not far from the shores of Lough Mask. Some years back Fred was kind enough to lend me the cottage for a whole month so that I could go over and see for myself exactly what Irish trout fishing was all about: it was a month I will never forget. The piece which follows extolling the delights of Irish fly fishing is by Fred himself:

I suppose the great charm for me must first of all be the fact that I am fishing for wild trout – truly wild fish that have nothing to do with stocking policies or stew ponds. That is becoming increasingly important to me and certainly the look of a wild brown trout is, in my opinion, quite unmatchable.

I think the next point of attraction is that fishing for the wild browns on Mask, Corrib or Conn must be the most difficult trout fishing I have ever experienced. The waters are colossal, so first of you have got to find feeding fish. But that's the easy part: the really difficult bit is working out some sort of strategy to catch them; I'm never in the least bit confident that I've got things right! In the evening perhaps you will get back to Cuslough and find that although you might not have caught anything at all, somebody else will have done

Fred Buller (second right) celebrates an angling get-together with Richard Walker to his left and Fred J. Taylor to his right.

The magnificent proportions of a big Irish fish.

well, and as the boats are being unloaded there will be trout a-plenty around him. Of course, everyone knows that a bag of trout is possible in theory but that in practice it is really hard to achieve, and I feel I'm always struggling, always up against it. In fact, I don't know anyone who really has a mastery over these wild Irish browns: no, perhaps that's not true, there are one or two quite exceptional Irish anglers who seem to know exactly what they're doing, what fly to use, what depth to fish it and how to work it in all the various conditions. Not like me, though. I've never got the fish at my mercy there and I'm never going to take them by the sackful. And perhaps the most frustrating thing of all is that if I do find something that works one day and gives me a modicum of success, I can be pretty well sure that the following day that technique or fly or whatever it was, will be next to useless! I know that's true of all fishing, but here it seems particularly pertinent.

An element of the pleasure I find in fishing these loughs is in handling the boat. The storms here often have to be seen to be believed and the waves can get really wild, and there's a real satisfaction in bringing the boat home safely and working it properly while you are fishing. If you can handle a boat on Mask in a heavy wind then you know you're something of a sailor – for me, this is a real part of the pleasure.

It's not only the fishing that makes Ireland so very dear to me, it's the people over there, too. I love getting across to Ireland, settling into my cottage, putting the boats out and then meeting up with familiar friends once again. It's very much a point of fishing over there that you meet on the island and have a brew-up with fishermen that you have known for years. You will see the little curl of smoke rise from an island and know that it's time for a break.

This socializing goes on at night, too, and when you are in Ballinrobe it's all part of the fishing to go after dinner to Luke's bar or Mick's bar or any of the other important fishing places in the town. There you'll see the Guinness being poured and standing to settle, and all the fishermen sitting around talking about their successes and their failures. You can talk seemingly all night until there's just time to snatch an hour or two's sleep before getting back onto the lough and putting into practice some of the ideas you've heard.

In short, these western Irish lakes for me are simply paradise: it's the fish and the people, the scenery and the way of life all rolled together into one glorious tapestry, and I'll never tire of the place.

And so the sun sets on us all.

INDEX

accessories 30
Albin 15
Alston, Reverend 45
Ardleigh Reservoir 8
Arkaig, Loch 135

Baby Doll 52
backing 28
Balinrobe 155
Barle, River 47
Beale, T 101
Bellers, V 93
Bennett, C 135
Bilbio 112
Black Pennell 112
Blae 'n' Black 112
Blagden Reservoir 103
boat fishing 98
Bob Fly 117
bottom contours 85
Bough Beech Reservoir 82
Boulton, T 89, 94
Bridgett, A 49
Buller, F 15, 155
Butchers 112

caddis 20
Caernarfon Arms 78
casting 38
char fishing 138
Chew Reservoir 8
Church, B 13
Clarke, B 55–6
clothing 31

Clunie, Loch 109
coarse fish 20
Conn, Lough 145
corixa 23
Cormorants 75
Corrib, Lough 145, 151

daddy-longlegs 23
daphnia 24
dapping 148, 150
Dog Nobblers 89
Dove, River 50
Dowdeswell Pike 80
downriggers 128
Downs, S 15
Draycote Reservoir 103
dry flies 35
Dunkeld 112

Edgefield Hall 8, 51
Elliott, D 150
emergers 35
Ennell, Lough 146
Exe, River 78
Eyebrook Reservoir 13

Falklands 16
Falkus, H 15
Farmoor Reservoir 102
fish finders 129
Fitt, J 85, 90
flies 33
fly lines 28
food of trout 20

Frost, W 15

Garich 120
Garry, Loch 143
Gent 52
Giles, N 15
Giles, W 88
Glaven, River 51
Grafham Reservoir 8
Green, D 73
Greenland 138
Goddard, M 108
Goldheads 37

Halford 10
hats 32
Heath, G 116
Hett, J 124
Hicklin-Bailey, J 19
Hinds Pit 47
Hollowell Reservoir 13
Houghton, Reverend 15

Inchlaggen Loch 144
indicators 49
Invicta 21, 112
Ivans, TC 11

Jurassic Lake 67

Kashmir 16
Kingsmill Moore, TC 148
Knight, J 88

leaders 29
Leary, D 81
livebaiting 130
Llandegfedd Reservoir 82
loch fishing 104
Lochans 119
Lochy, Loch 116, 119
Lomond, Loch 105

lures 34
Lyng 80, 83

Macdonald, J 131
March Browns 112
Mask, Lough 126
mayfly 60
McKelvie, K 15
Melvin, Lough 15
midges 22
Miles, T 84
Miller, R 88
Missionary Lure 13
Montana 16

Ness, Loch 139
New Zealand 16
Norfolk Fly Fishers' Lake 8
North 15
Northampton Style 13
nymphs 35

Ogborne, C 13
Oich, Loch 116
Owel, Lough 148

Parkinson, P 25
Pawson, T 87
pike 80
polaroid glasses 43
Polystickles 21

Quoich, Loch 109

Rannoch, Loch 109
Ravensthorpe Reservoir 13
reel 27
Regan, T 15
Rickards, B 134
Robins, M & A 49
rods 25
Rutland Reservoir 8

safety 32
Sandys, R 88
Sawyer, F 11
Sheeling, Lake 145
Sheringham, HT 11
Shrive, D 12
Skues 10
Stone, P 71

Taylor, FJ 11
terrestrials 35
Tintwhistle Reservoir 7
trolling 127
trout, brook 18
   brown 15

ferox 124
rainbow 17

waders 31
Walker, R 8, 11
wet flies 35
Wheeler, A 15
Wilson, D 36
Wimbleball Reservoir 102
Windermere, Lake 126
winter fly fishing 79

Yarrell 15

Zulus 112